S0-ARO-810

⇉ Endorsements ⇇

It is one thing to know facts about God in your head, but quite another to know Him intimately, personally, and in a close heart-to-heart relationship. *I Know His Name* will enable you to develop such a closeness with God by allowing you to get to know Him through His many names used in Scripture. Wendy has an uncanny ability to combine Bible passages, personal stories, and practical application in a way that expands your faith and strengthens your walk with God. If you are serious about taking your relationship with your Creator to a place of deep connection, read and then live out the truths of this book!

> —**Karen Ehman**, *New York Times* bestselling author of *Keep It Shut* and eight other books; national speaker with Proverbs 31 Ministries; wife and mom of three

My dear friend Wendy Blight has taught me so much about prayer and God's love through her own grace and love for others. There is no doubt that her book *I Know His Name* is going to be a huge blessing to so many and grow His kingdom even bigger.

> —**Emily Maynard**, Author of *I Said Yes: My Story of Heartbreak, Redemption, and True Love*

What a wonderful study! I was so blessed by how Wendy, in such a practical, helpful way, guides us through the names of God, what they mean, and how that knowledge will empower our relationship with the Lord. You too will be blessed!

> —**Jennifer Rothschild**, Author of *Lessons I Learned in the Dark*; *Self Talk, Soul Talk*; and *Invisible*; founder of Fresh Grounded Faith events and womensministry.net

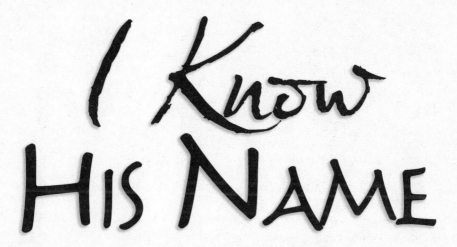

I Know His Name

DISCOVERING POWER in the NAMES OF GOD

WENDY BLIGHT

AUTHOR OF *Living So That*

THOMAS NELSON
Since 1798

NASHVILLE   MEXICO CITY   RIO DE JANEIRO

© 2015 by Wendy Blight

All rights reserved. No portion of this book may be reproduced, stored in a retrieval system, or transmitted in any form or by any means—electronic, mechanical, photocopy, recording, scanning, or other—except for brief quotations in critical reviews or articles, without the prior written permission of the publisher.

Published in Nashville, Tennessee, by Nelson Books, an imprint of Thomas Nelson. Nelson Books and Thomas Nelson are registered trademarks of HarperCollins Christian Publishing, Inc.

Author represented by Erik S. Wolgemuth; Wolgemuth and Associates, Inc.

Page design and layout: Crosslin Creative

Thomas Nelson titles may be purchased in bulk for educational, business, fund-raising, or sales promotional use. For information, please e-mail SpecialMarkets@ ThomasNelson.com.

Unless otherwise indicated, Scripture quotations are taken *The Voice*™ translation, copyright © 2012 Ecclesia Bible Society. Used by permission. All rights reserved.

Scripture quotations marked NIV are taken from The Holy Bible, *New International Version*®, *NIV*®. Copyright © 1973, 1978, 1984, 2011 by Biblica, Inc.® Used by permission. All rights reserved worldwide.

Quotations marked NKJV are taken from the New King James Version. Copyright © 1982 by Thomas Nelson, Inc. Used by permission. All rights reserved.

Quotations marked NLT are taken from the *Holy Bible, New Living Translation*, copyright © 1996, 2004. Used by permission of Tyndale House Publishers, Inc., Wheaton, Illinois. All rights reserved.

Quotations marked KJV are from the King James Version (public domain).

ISBN 978-0-7180-0420-0

Printed in the United States of America

Dedication

To my Charlotte Bible Study girls. One of your questions (the day we prayed at the bowling alley) birthed this book. Your zeal to study God's Word continually challenges me to venture to new and deeper places in Scripture. Your constant prayers, love, and encouragement bless me more than you will ever know.

⇒⇒ Acknowledgments ⇐⇐

With deep appreciation, I thank the cherished friends and family listed below:

Monty—You are my best friend, and I love doing life with you.

Lauren and Bo—You light up my life with joy and laughter. Being your mom is my most favorite job in the whole world.

Robin Phillips—You said yes to *I Know His Name*. Thank you for believing in me and investing your time and exceptional talents in this book.

Lisa Sheltra—Dear friend and editor extraordinaire. Thank you for pouring hours and hours into this manuscript to ensure its biblical integrity and excellence.

Bobbie Wolgemuth—You loved me like one of your own. You spoke, sang, and prayed precious truths into my life in the midst of your own toughest battle. This past year, you went to be with Jesus. My heart aches that I will never again hear your sweet voice this side of heaven. But I hold fast to the hope that I will see you again.

Erik and Robert Wolgemuth—Thank you for your wise counsel and helping me navigate the business side of what we do.

Lisa Allen—You are a precious gift from God.

My Proverbs Thirty-One OBS family and First 5 Writing Team—You weave God's truth into my life in such beautiful ways and make ministry so much fun.

HarperCollins Christian Publishing—Thank you for investing in this book and coming alongside me, and so many other authors, to equip women to draw closer to God through His living and active Word.

Contents

➤➤ Introduction ◄◄

Welcome to *I Know His Name: Discovering Power in the Names of God*. I am excited that you have chosen to join me on this adventure through God's Word. Be confident, my friend, that you will meet God in a fresh way in the pages of His Word and the beautiful messages in this book. He makes a great promise in Isaiah 55:11, and I want you to keep that promise tucked in your heart: "So it is when I declare something. My word will go out and not return to Me empty, but it will do what I wanted; it will accomplish what I determined." During our time together, we will dive into deep waters and unveil new truths and promises about our God that will transform how we pray and interact with Him from this day forward.

I Know His Name can be read individually or with a small group. I encourage a small group setting because it allows for accountability and rich discussions with other women about what you have learned.

You will notice that several translations are used throughout the book, mainly The Voice and the New International Version. Even if you don't own either of these translations, you will be able to complete the lessons without difficulty. In fact, using various translations while you study God's Word will only enhance your understanding.

I Know His Name leads you through five chapters, combining personal stories with Old and New Testament stories and Scriptures. Each chapter opens with prayer and a memory verse. I encourage you to pray the prayer as soon as you begin the lesson. Remember, the Holy Spirit is your teacher. God's Word comes alive in our hearts when the Holy Spirit interprets what God is speaking to us. Praying invites God's Spirit into your reading and learning, and prepares your heart to receive all that God has for you. And please don't let the memory verses intimidate you. If you can remember the words of your favorite tune or the lines of your favorite movie, you will be able to memorize these verses!

Each lesson includes a teaching, a section for Digging Deeper into God's Word, and a section to Apply It to your own life. There is space for you to write your answers, but I encourage you to get a journal or notebook to use as well. Designate a special time each day to complete your reading and study. Ask the Lord to help you make it a priority. He will be faithful.

The questions in the Apply It section are intended to help you practically apply what you are learning. When you answer them, think about what you have learned, the ways God has spoken to you, and what He asked you to do in response to what you have heard.

A five-session video study is also available in both DVD and downloadable formats (sold separately). If you or your group chooses to utilize the video teaching in addition to this book, be sure to complete the book chapter before watching the video.

On our adventure together, we will unveil God's character, name by name, including:

▶ *Elohim*: The One Who Created You

▶ *El Roi*: The One Who Sees You

▶ *Jehovah Nissi*: The One Who Stands Guard Over You

▶ *Jehovah Rapha*: The One Who Heals You

▶ *Jehovah Shalom*: The One Who Gives You Peace

▶ *All-Consuming Fire*: The One Who Is Jealous for You (An All-Consuming Fire)

▶ *El Elyon*: The One Who Is the God Most High

▶ *Abba Father*: The One Who Is Your Father

As you open your Bible, know that God breathed each and every word; then men inspired by God's own Spirit wrote them down. Although written by human hands, each word is divinely inspired, thereby reliable, infallible, and true.

It's not about increasing our head knowledge. We are studying God's Word so that we can know Him better and so that God can change our hearts and our lives! So, friend, surrender your heart and your schedule to Him and join me for a great adventure!

Message from My Heart

"Bible study field day!" we exclaimed as we piled into a few cars and headed out for a fun day of bowling and fellowship. Our morning was filled with lots of laughter and, yes, a little bit of competitiveness. But that all changed in one moment when one of our sisters received a call that her husband had been taken to the hospital for emergency surgery. She rushed out the door with two of our friends, and a few of us called out that we would join her after we prayed. We gathered in a circle, and I opened our prayer with the words "Jehovah Rapha," which means "God the Healer" in Hebrew. Eyes closed, hands clasped, tears falling, we stood united in heart and Spirit and prayed for God to heal my friend's husband. Unbeknownst to me, one woman had opened her eyes, elbowed the woman next to her, and whispered, "Why is Wendy praying to another God? Does she believe in another God that I don't know?"

The day my friend shared this conversation, it was an eye-opening moment. I realized that in the years I had been teaching Bible study, I had never shared the fact that Scripture contains *hundreds* of names for God and that those names speak to the vastness of His character and how He works on our behalf. I knew then that I needed to share that knowledge with as many people as I could. Because, friend, the more deeply we explore our God, the more we move from simply knowing *about* Him to truly *knowing* Him.

Some of you grew up knowing and believing in God, and He is familiar to you. Others of you are new believers to whom God is a bit of a mystery. But what matters to me is that you are here, and I believe with all my heart that God drew you here.

I am so grateful to come alongside you on this journey of unveiling God. I hope you feel prompted to ask lots of questions, because questions are good! God has a divinely appointed message for you and questions He wants to answer for you. Be assured that He will meet you wherever you are and unfold great and marvelous truths about Himself and His creation.

I pray that the pages of this book will empower you to experience God in fresh new ways. To uncover life-changing revelations regarding His splendor and majesty, His sovereignty and power, His love and protection, and His faithfulness and goodness. You may be familiar with these words and understand their meaning. But it's my desire that through our time together, you will study them, savor them, believe them, claim them, pray them, and live confidently in them every day of your life.

Friend, God delights in us and created us for inconceivable joy and fulfillment! Listen to His invitation: "Taste of His goodness; see how wonderful the Eternal truly is" (Psalm 34:8a). May He engage all our senses with every turn of the page.

As we unwrap the mysteries of God's Word, we will experience the fullness of His goodness and the sweetness of His presence in every facet of our lives. Together let's digest each and every truth, soaking in them until they become part and parcel of who we are, what we think, and how we act.

Are you excited about our adventure? I know I am, so let's jump right in!

CHAPTER ONE

Elohim: The One Who Created You

Prayer:

O God, I'm so excited for this journey on which I'm about to embark. I'm thirsting not only to know more about You, but also to know You more. God, through the power of Your Holy Spirit, help me to discover who You truly are. Open my eyes to see, my ears to hear, and my heart to understand eternal mysteries that only You can reveal on this exciting adventure. Give me the discipline to do my work, the perseverance to continue when I want to give up, and the mind to practically apply all that I learn. Enable me to taste and see that You are good. Show me marvelous things from Your Word. Reveal Your majesty, show me Your glory, and draw me so close to Your heart that I feel, down to the marrow of my bones, that You are the All-Consuming Fire! I ask all this in Jesus' Name, Amen.

Part One:
In the Beginning

> **Memory Verse:** In the beginning, God created *everything:*
> the heavens *above* and the *earth below. Here's what happened.*
>
> —Genesis 1:1

The Word declares that our God is a personal God and a loving and forgiving Father. He demands justice, yet extends grace. He is kind and compassionate and allows for free will, but mandates that this free will has consequences when wrongly exercised. However, because of His grace, in the midst of those consequences, God extends mercy and promises to never leave us or forsake us.

Do you ever wonder what our world would be like if everyone knew our God in this way? I do ... often.

The notion that God has continued to impress upon my heart is this: if we are to introduce others to the God whom we know and love, then we must know Him better. When I first had this thought, hard questions followed. *Wendy, how well do you really know Me? My heart, My character, My names, and the attributes those names represent?*

I must confess—I did not. When I first started reading the Bible, I noticed that the writers referred to God by other names now and then. But I did not pay much attention or question why, and often I could not even pronounce the names! As I studied the Bible more, I learned that each name *meant* something; sometimes the name pointed to an aspect of God's character, and other times it pointed to how He relates to His people. Over time, I could recite many of those names and pray them eloquently, but I really didn't understand all of them or know where each name originated.

So I immersed myself in the pages of His Word once again, this time inviting God to unveil Himself to me in a fresh way. I prayed, "Show me who You are, God, and why I should care. Reveal to me why You are worthy of being called the One True God; why I should unabashedly love and serve You and You alone. Decipher Your names. Make known Your character. Help me know You better so I can live and walk in the image in which You created me."

As I poured myself into the Scriptures, God answered my prayers. And the more I approached God's Word with an open heart, the more I fell in love with God's wonderful names—the names that reveal the vastness of His character. The names that affirm the work He does on our behalf.

Friend, the more deeply we explore our God, the more we are able to move beyond simply knowing *about* Him to truly *knowing* Him. And as that love grows and our relationship strengthens, God settles into that special place—reserved solely for Him—that He created in our hearts. We become a living, breathing vessel through whom God can work in this world. He transforms our hearts, and through our changed hearts God can change the world.

> *The more deeply we explore our God, the more we are able to move beyond simply knowing about Him to truly knowing Him.*

Our newfound knowledge will give us privileged access into God's heart and open new ways for us to experience Him in quiet time, prayer, and worship.

So let's turn our attention to *Elohim* (pronounced el-o-heem), the God who created us.

We find our first name of God in Genesis 1. In an English-language Bible we see the word *God*. But in the original Hebrew language, the word was *Elohim*. The word *el* is a generic word for god. It refers to our God as well as other, pagan gods. The writers of the Bible added the word *im* to the end of this generic name. This is like adding an "s" to the end of a word in English; it makes the word plural.

So the noun *Elohim* is plural, but it is always used with a singular verb. What does this mean? It means *Elohim* signifies one triune God, not many gods. This unique use of the plural *Elohim* to refer to one, individual god is unique to the God of the Bible. No other God has the name *Elohim*.

Why is this significant? Because it indicates a unity *and* diversity within the nature of God. The Hebrew language often pluralized nouns to express greatness and multiple attributes. With the name *Elohim*, this unity and diversity captures the doctrine of the Trinity—one God in three persons: God the Father, God the Son, and God the Holy Spirit.

Though the exact meaning of *Elohim* is not known, the name itself incorporates the idea of strength and power and speaks to the supremacy of God as He reveals Himself through His creation. We find it in the opening words of Genesis 1: "In the beginning, God created *everything*: the heavens *above* and the earth *below* ..." (Genesis 1:1a).

Digging Deeper

In the beginning God created. Our universe does not exist by accident. God acted freely and intentionally with each word He spoke. He executed each stage of creation's design. Just look around you—the glorious beauty that lies before you has been carefully crafted by a living, personal, creative God! *Elohim* purposefully placed earth in its exact location and deposited each one of His created people on that earth at a specially ordained time and place in order to accomplish His purposes!

Read Acts 17:24–27. How do Luke's words confirm the truth that God is Creator?

Throughout Scripture, God's Word affirms and confirms that He is the Creator. Read the following verses and share what you learn about *Elohim*.

1. Psalm 8:3–9

2. Proverbs 3:19

3. Isaiah 40:26

—》》 Apply It

Our God has done great and unsearchable things beyond our comprehension. He brought into existence every natural wonder the eye can see: every twinkling star, every delicate snowflake, every drop of rain, every billowy cloud, every crisp cool day, every roaring sea, every clap of thunder, every bolt of lightning, every majestic

mountain—all gifts shaped and fashioned by our Creator. *Elohim*'s invisible qualities echo throughout our world: "From the beginning, creation in its magnificence enlightens us to His nature. Creation itself makes His undying power and divine identity clear, even though they are invisible; and it voids the excuses *and ignorant claims* of these people" (Romans 1:20).

Elohim dictates the rising and the setting of the sun. He sets the boundaries of the sea. The stars rise and fall at His command. Nothing, absolutely nothing, has been or ever will be that His hand has not created.

Take some time today to thank God for His creation. Look outside your window. Remember the sights and sounds from any of your trips to the mountains or the beach. Praise Him for all He has created for your enjoyment and pleasure! Write your prayer of praise in the space provided.

Part Two:
Creator of Heaven and Earth

> **Memory Verse:** In the beginning, God created *everything:* the heavens *above* and the *earth below. Here's what happened."*
>
> —Genesis 1:1

Let's revisit Genesis 1 as we probe deeper into the word *create* and what exactly God created "in the beginning."

Reread Genesis 1:1.

"In the beginning" refers to a specific point in time. While Genesis 1:1 is the starting point of creation, God existed before that time. He is an infinite being without beginning and without end (Revelation 21:6; 22:13). But in Genesis 1:1, God initiated a work that is measured by time as we understand it.

The word *create*, as used here, translates from the Hebrew word *bara*.[1] By definition, a deity name is always the subject or the implied subject of this verb, meaning it refers solely to divine work. This has profound theological significance because it means that any activity associated with this word is inherently divine, initiated by God and God alone. All other verbs for "creating" allow a much broader range of meaning and can have both divine and human subjects.

Most scholars agree that *create*, as used here, expresses the notion of creation out of nothing. In other words, there was no preexistent matter from which our earth was produced. The light, waters, dry land, and seas created in Genesis 1:3–10 were made out of nothing, formed at God's command and then filled with God's created things.

Read Isaiah 45:18. How does this verse speak about creation?

>>> Digging Deeper

Human logic teaches that you cannot create something out of nothing. Our understanding of the laws of nature governing the universe make such a thing impossible. But by the power of our Almighty God, such things are possible. In fact, God's Word explicitly states that with God *all* things are possible (Matthew 19:26; Luke 18:27).

How does God create something out of nothing? What exactly happened in Genesis 1? To answer this, we must first know what our world looked like at the time of creation.

Read Genesis 1:2 and John 1:1–2. Describe the condition of the earth at the time of creation. Who was present?

In the beginning the earth was formless, empty, and dark (from the Hebrew words *tohuw, bohuw,* and *choshek*). *Tohuw* means "to lie waste, a desolation, a worthless thing." It also means "confusion, without order."[2] *Bohuw* means "to be empty."[3] *Choshek* means "darkness, dark (as withholding light)."[4] This darkness surrounded a desolate, unformed mass. There was absolutely no light. It was out of this chaos, this immense mass of matter, that God created the earth upon which we walk today.

Biblical scholars debate exactly how creation occurred and the actual number of days or years that it took. Some theologians theorize that there were actually two creations. They base this on Genesis 1:2, which says that God was present in a mass of unformed matter before He initiated His first day of creative work, which is described in Genesis 1:3. Genesis 1:2 says, "The Spirit of God was hovering over the empty waters." They contend that Genesis 1:2 describes the first stage of God's creative process, initially unformed and unfilled, and that Genesis 1:3 relays the second phase, His intentional, purposeful process of forming and filling the earth.

While these are fascinating debates, for our purposes this distinction is irrelevant. We want to focus on the first few verses of Genesis 1, which teach that at a certain point in time, God's Holy Spirit—the power that parted the Red Sea, the power that raised Jesus from the dead—brought shape, order, and light to a formless, chaotic mass.

What do you think the universe felt and looked like before God's Spirit began His creative work? Describe your image of the earth before God said in Genesis 1:3, "Let there be light."

The words in Genesis 1:3–25 generate still more controversy among biblical scholars. Scripture teaches that God created our earth in six days. The probing question is whether this refers to six literal days as we know them. Some scholars argue that the days in Genesis 1 represent six literal days as measured by our modern-day calendar. Others argue the days represent eons of time. Still others argue the referenced days are merely a literary device and have nothing to do with the actual length of time that passed.

🖋 **Read Genesis 1:3–25.** What words or phrases might lead to the conclusion that God completed His creation in six literal days? (See also Exodus 20:11.)

🖋 **Read 2 Peter 3:8.** What does this verse say about creation?

Although we will not dwell on the answers to either of these questions because there is no certain resolution, they are interesting to think about. But what is certain is that Genesis 1 makes it quite clear that we live in a personal world created by a loving God, who brought forth something from nothing ... who brought life from death ... who made full from empty. And the best news of all is our God wants to do the very same for each one of us.

> *We live in a personal world created by a loving God, who brought forth something from nothing ... who brought life from death ... who made full from empty. And the best news of all is our God wants to do the very same for each one of us.*

Now, let's explore God's creative activity during those first six days.

Reread Genesis 1:3. Describe what happened on day one.

As we study God's creative process, we find distinct steps. First, God spoke. Second, what God spoke came to be. Third, God evaluated His work and commented on it. Fourth, God named what He created. Finally, God established evening and morning, a beginning and end to each day.

Do you see this exact process in each of the first five days of creation?

Did you find any differences between the days? If so, what are they and in what ways do you find them significant?

Did you notice God created each thing "according to its kind"? The root word here is *miyn* in Hebrew. It means "to portion out, to sort."[5] God designed each creature in a distinctive way. He did not create one or two types of creatures and intend for them to evolve into other forms. Each species, whether plant or animal, had its own distinct features, purpose, and role in God's created order. The vegetation (1:11–12), the living creatures of the sea (1:21), the winged birds (1:21), and the living creatures on the land (1:24) were all created "according to their kind." What God's Word makes clear is this: God did not create an amoeba that eventually evolved into a fish or a monkey that over time turned into a man. He fashioned each creature as a distinct "kind." What a creative and awesome God we have!

> *God did not create an amoeba that eventually evolved into a fish or a monkey that over time turned into a man. He fashioned each creature as a distinct "kind."*

We see God's incredible handiwork displayed most magnificently when we next meet the crowning work of His creation, mankind.

Read Genesis 1:26–27. Did you notice God changed His creative process? Reread Genesis 1:26 and share how it opens differently from God's other creative processes.

This time God said, "Let *us* make mankind in *our* image, in *our* likeness" (Genesis 1:26a). Creating people became a joint effort, a creative work done by God the Father, His Son, and the Holy Spirit. This is the first hint of the Trinity we see in the Bible.

Read Genesis 1:27 and write it below.

These carefully chosen words make it very clear that we did not evolve from any kind of animal. God made us in His image and likeness. *Image*, translated from the Hebrew word *tselem*, means "shape, resemblance, shadow."[6] *Likeness*, translated from the Hebrew *dmuwth*, means "shape, fashion, model" and signifies the original after which a thing is patterned.[7]

Friend, lean in close and soak up these words. Our heavenly Father shaped and patterned us after Himself. By His very hand, He formed every inch of our forefather, Adam, from the top of his head to the tips of his toes. He gave Adam a heart to love and feel, a mind to think and comprehend, a tongue to speak and praise, emotions to laugh and cry, and talents to work and serve. God makes it very clear in His Word—we are *not* like every other created creature! He made us in His image, in His likeness, with His heart and His mind. As my pastor says, we carry the divine DNA of our Creator!

> *Our heavenly Father shaped and patterned us after Himself.*

Jump ahead for a moment to Genesis 2:7 to find the specifics of how God created man.

Read the words of Genesis 2:7: "One day the Eternal God scooped dirt out of the ground, sculpted it into *the shape we call* human, breathed the breath that gives life into the nostrils of the human, and the human became a living soul." From what did God make man?

 Why do you think God made a man out of the dust of the earth?

 After *Elohim* scooped the dirt and sculpted the dirt into a formed being, what did He do in Genesis 2:7?

Apply It

I want you to grasp the weight of the words in Genesis 2:7! God breathed a piece of Himself into Adam. God gave Adam, and He still gives us today, the breath of life!

 What does it mean to you that you are created in the image of God? What are some attributes of God (compassion, love, grace, justice, wisdom, creativity, truth) that you see in yourself?

Part Three:
Adam and Eve

Memory Verse: In the beginning, God created *everything:* the heavens *above* and the *earth below. Here's what happened.*

—Genesis 1:1

How are you coming along with your memory verse? Does it hold more meaning as you unveil the creative side of our God, *Elohim*?

Genesis 1 isn't the only place we find evidence that God is Creator. We find further affirmation throughout both the Old and New Testaments. Isaiah 45:18 reminds us, "For this is what the LORD says—he who created the heavens, he is God; he who fashioned and made the earth, he founded it; he did not create it to be empty, but formed it to be inhabited—he says: I am the LORD, and there is no other" (NIV).

Elohim formed and shaped our universe. Psalm 148:5–6 says, "Let all things *join together in a concert of* praise to the name of the Eternal, for He gave the command and they were created. He put them in their places *to stay* forever—He declared it so, and it is final."

Read Psalm 104 and write down your thoughts and feelings about what the psalmist shares about creation.

Both Psalm 19 and Romans 1 explain that God's creation is a reflection, a "wordless" message, about how God is the Creator of heaven and earth.

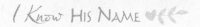
🖋 **Read Psalm 19:1–6 and Romans 1:18–20.** The author of Psalm 19 and Paul, the author of Romans, both speak of creation itself as compelling evidence that God is Creator of all things, but for different reasons. What are those reasons?

⇝ Digging Deeper

God labored for six days before He created mankind. God wanted to prepare a beautiful place for Adam and Eve. So before their arrival, He readied the earth by filling it with living things for their nourishment, use, and enjoyment. And, finally, at the end of the sixth day, God brought both Adam and Eve into being.

God's creation story paved the way for another story—the story of relationships. More specifically, the relationship between Adam, and Eve. God created Adam first. He knew Adam would be lonely and would need a companion. But not one of his created creatures suited that role. Adam needed someone special, someone created just for him. So *Elohim* caused Adam to fall into a deep sleep. While he was sleeping, God removed one of Adam's ribs and from it fashioned a woman—Eve, God's final creation. I like to say He saved the best for last!

God then presented the woman to Adam, who named her, saying, "At last, a *suitable companion, a perfect partner.* Bone of my bones. Flesh from my flesh. I will call this one 'woman' as *an eternal reminder that* she was taken out of man" (Genesis 2:23).

Eve had special significance because God created her to be Adam's helpmate, to come alongside him to rule over earth (Genesis 1:26). They walked and talked with God every day, safe and secure in their relationship with their Creator. He provided for their every need. God gave Adam and Eve the responsibility to care for and manage His creation. He equipped them, uniquely in all creation, with a mind and will of their own so they could do just that.

God gave Adam and Eve everything they needed; they lacked for nothing physically, spiritually, or emotionally. A.W. Tozer wrote of man's heart at this stage: "In the deep heart of the man was a shrine where none but God was worthy to come. Within him was God; without, a thousand gifts which God had showered upon him."[8]

God placed only one restriction on the happy couple. They were not to eat from the tree in the center of the garden in which they lived. Sadly, Eve made the mistake of wandering near the forbidden tree. Then Adam and Eve used their free will to defy the very God who created them.

Read Genesis 3:1–7. What happened when Eve wandered over to the tree?

Read Genesis 3:21–24. What was God's response?

Adam and Eve chose disobedience and fell from *Elohim*'s grace. He issued severe punishments to them, including the loss of their home, a sentence of hard work, and a promise of sorrow, pain, conflict, and ultimately death.

Adam and Eve's one rebellious act—called "the fall" because they fell from God's grace—downloaded sin (the tendency to rebel against God) into every generation of people thereafter, forever affecting the relationship between God and man, between man and

God's creation, between husbands and wives, and among siblings, families, communities, and nations.

Sin "introduced complications and has made [the] very gifts of God a potential source of ruin to the soul."[9] Sadly, Adam and Eve desired the gifts more than they desired the Giver. A.W. Tozer writes, "Within the human heart 'things' have taken over. Men now have by nature no peace within their hearts, for God is crowned there no longer, but there in the moral dusk stubborn and aggressive usurpers fight among themselves for first place on the throne."[10]

Because Adam and Eve's sin passed from one generation to the next, "things" have taken over our hearts. We too covet "things" more than God.

> Adam and Eve's one rebellious act—called "the fall" because they fell from God's grace—downloaded sin (the tendency to rebel against God) into every generation of people thereafter.

⟩⟩ Apply It

Because God loved His creation and longed to be back in relationship with them, He continually intervened in their lives and sought to show them their sin and draw them into repentance. Sadly, God's children responded with stubbornness. Though at times some repented and turned their hearts back to God, as a whole they repeated the sins of Adam and Eve. And, if we're honest with ourselves, we'll admit that sometimes we behave just like the people we read about in the Bible. I have good news for you though! *Elohim* had a plan, and that plan was fulfilled in the gift of our Savior, Jesus Christ. So, let me challenge you to examine your own heart today.

Because God loved His creation and longed to be back in relationship with them, He continually intervened in their lives and sought to show them their sin and draw them into repentance.

What good gifts from God do you desire more than the Giver? Take a few minutes to reflect on this, and then make a list of anything that you currently desire more than God.

Write a prayer asking God to help you desire Him and love His Word more than anything else.

Part Four: Created in His Image

Memory Verse: In the beginning, God created *everything:* the heavens *above* and the *earth below. Here's what happened."*

—Genesis 1:1

God speaks in the most unique and unexpected ways. One afternoon, my daughter and I joined several of our girlfriends for lunch. As it is when you gather with friends, laughter filled our time together, so much so that, at my age, it prompted a quick trip to the ladies' room. As I closed the door in the stall, an advertisement for a plastic surgeon caught my eye: "Define yourself through the hands and eyes of a true artist."

The words pierced my heart. The joy and laughter that had filled my heart moments before vanished as I realized that there are women searching so desperately for their identity that they would look for it on the back of a bathroom door. I thought too of how God's heart must ache when one of His beautiful creations—a woman He created with strength, dignity, beauty, and unique purpose—hastily adds this doctor's number to her contacts. Sadly, this is where our culture has led us.

What our world has lost sight of—and what this doctor seems to have flippantly and arrogantly tossed aside—is the fact that there is only one true Artist. His name: *Elohim.* He alone is the Creator of human life; He alone is the source of our identity.

⟩⟩ Digging Deeper

Genesis 1 has taught us that God, in the first six days of creation, created the heavens and the earth and filled them with an incredible assortment of celestial bodies, geographical wonders, plants, and animals. At the end of that sixth day, God handcrafted the first two human beings, Adam and Eve. But God didn't stop there; He continues to create life. He handcrafted each one of us. One of my favorite psalms beautifully portrays this truth.

Read **Psalm 139:13–16.** What does this passage teach you?

You are fearfully and wonderfully made by *Elohim*! Do you believe that God created every part of you—your body, your mind, your heart, your spirit, your soul? How does this make you feel?

Read **Ephesians 2:10.**

God did not create us all from the same mold. We're not all designed to look like a Victoria's Secret model or a box-office movie starlet—and that's perfectly okay! Ephesians 2:10 (NIV) declares we are God's "workmanship." The Greek word for *workmanship* is *poiema*, which means "a product," something created from scratch.[11] From this Greek word we derive our English word *poem*. A poem is a work of art crafted with extraordinary skill. Friend, you too are a work of art! A supreme achievement. A work completely created and fashioned by God's hand. A vessel for His use and for His glory.

God did not create us all from the same mold.

All too often, we women struggle to believe this. We sometimes see ourselves only as a knotted, tangled mess—like the underside of my grandmother's cross-stitch patterns. But when I flip the stitched work over, I see the beauty of the finished product, woven together in an intricate pattern, perfectly crafted to bring joy and delight to all observers. That beauty was there all along, but I just couldn't see it until I changed my perspective. So let's revisit Genesis 1 for some answers on how to change our self-perception and to combat the lies we too often believe.

Do you believe that you truly are God's masterpiece? If not, why?

What lies have you believed about yourself that might hinder you from seeing yourself as God's masterpiece? Write down these things. Then ask God to help you to replace those lies with the truth of His Word.

Genesis 1:26 explains how God created us. Here God says, "Now let Us conceive *a new creation*—humanity—*made* in Our image, *fashioned* according to Our likeness. And let *Us grant* them authority over all the earth—the fish in the sea and the birds in the sky, the domesticated animals and the *small* creeping creatures on the earth."

Did you notice that God said "let *Us*"? Who is "Us"? It refers to the Trinity—the three persons of the Trinity joined together to fashion God's final creation. Human beings, the crown of God's creation, are the handiwork of God the Father, God the Son, *and*

God the Holy Spirit. This truth distinguishes us from every other creature God made.

In fact, this verse (Genesis 1:26) teaches that we are not only distinguished from the other creatures but also given responsibility. But for what? (See also Psalm 8:3–6.)

Earlier, we studied the words *image* and *likeness*. Let's return to these terms to go a bit deeper. *Image* translates from the Hebrew word *tselem* and means "an illusion, a resemblance." *Strong's Concordance* says God made man in His image, "reflecting some of His own perfections: perfect in knowledge, righteousness, and holiness, and with dominion over the creatures."[12] *Likeness* translates from the Hebrew word *dmuwth* and signifies in this verse "the original after which a thing is patterned."[13]

What does it mean that we are created in the image of God?

God is quite clear. Adam was not made in the likeness of any creature that went before him but in the likeness of his Creator. God created man from the dust of the earth, shaped him with His hands, breathed His very breath into him, and then imprinted His image on his heart, mind, soul, and body.

We bear the image of God. Cling to this truth and treasure it always in your heart. We share, though imperfectly and finitely, in God's nature. He imparted His identity, emotions, personality, creativity, wisdom, love, holiness, and justice into each one of us.

We bear the image of God. Cling to this truth and treasure it always in your heart.

Do you know what this means? It means *you* are His child, created in His image, valuable and worthy in His sight for all eternity!

Read Genesis chapter 2. What are some ways you see God expressing His love for the man, Adam, whom He created in His image (vv. 9, 15–17, 20–21, 23)?

How are we created in the image of God? Three ways strike me in particular:

The Mind of God

God endowed us with intellectual ability far superior to that of any animal. He gave us a mind capable of hearing and assimilating His Word. He gave us emotions capable of responding to His love. And He gave us wills enabling us to choose whether to obey His Word.

Share ways you exhibit this God-given intellectual ability in your everyday life.

The Character of God

God created us to be holy as He is holy. Adam and Eve, in their holiness, experienced perfect communion with the Father. They lived and walked in God's moral perfection. We know this because in Genesis 1:31, God affirmed that everything He had made was "very good." It was only because of the fall that Adam and Eve, and all mankind, lost moral perfection. But God's holiness, His character, is still embedded in us. And through the power of His Holy Spirit, by which we were sealed when we accepted Him as our Lord and Savior, we can live and walk in that holy character.

Some would say our conscience keeps us from choosing evil over good. What is it really that keeps believers from succumbing to temptation and disobeying God? How does God speak to you when you find yourself in this place of temptation?

Share some of the ways we can be light to the world by showing our lost and dark world that we are created in God's image.

The Fellowship of God

Before time began, God existed not alone but in fellowship with the Son and the Holy Spirit. God, who *is* love, desires love and relationship and created us to desire the same. Within each of us is a space made by Him, for Him. When He takes up residence in that space, He intends to fill it so completely that nothing else can ever satisfy. God also created us for fellowship with other people.

Read Proverbs 27:17. Then take a moment to think about the people with whom you are most closely in fellowship. Are those relationships God-honoring? Is your fellowship driving you to a deeper love of your Savior or hindering you from growing in your faith?

God has imprinted His image on us in a unique way, hand-crafted and gifted each of us with spiritual gifts and distinct talents. Never forget that *you* are the *only you* there has ever been or ever will be. God has a special plan for your life, and it's one that only you can fulfill.

> *God has a special plan for your life, and it's one that only you can fulfill.*

We should never again look at ourselves (or others) as being without value or worth. Yes, Adam and Eve marred the image of God engraved on their hearts, and yes, they passed that damaged likeness on to their descendants, including you and me (Romans 5:12). But this fact does not nullify the truth that we bear God's image. It just means that we bear the scars of sin as well.

Even though we are born with a sinful nature, we find good news tucked into Genesis 3:15. God punished the serpent for interfering in the garden and drawing His children into temptation: "I will make you and your brood enemies of the woman and all her children; the woman's child will stomp your head, and you will strike his heel."

God warned of the perpetual animosity between Satan's forces and God's children. The first offspring (seed) of Eve was Cain, followed by all of humanity, including Christ. The offspring of the serpent includes demons, those who serve his kingdom of darkness, those whose father is the devil (John 8:44). God's punishment prophesied that, although Satan would continually launch attacks against mankind (strike at his heel), the seed of Eve—one Seed in particular—Christ, would deliver Satan's fatal blow (stomp his head).

God loves us so much that, even in those first days of creation, He set a plan in place to redeem us, to restore all that Adam and Eve lost. A plan that called for His Son to give His life for ours. That redemption began a process whereby, through salvation, God restores in each one of us the original unblemished image of God.

Read Ephesians 4:24. How does it speak to what we are talking about here?

Read aloud the following passage from Ephesians 2:4–9:

> But God, with the *unfathomable* richness of His love and mercy focused on us, united us with the Anointed One and infused our lifeless souls with life—even though we were buried under mountains of sin—and saved us by His grace. He raised us up with Him and seated us in the heavenly realms with our *beloved* Jesus the Anointed, *the Liberating King. He did this for a reason*: so that for all eternity we will stand as a living testimony to the incredible riches of His grace and kindness that He freely gives to us by uniting us with Jesus the Anointed. For it's by God's grace that you have been saved. You receive it through faith. It was not our plan or our effort. It is God's gift, *pure and simple*. You didn't earn it, *not one of us did*, so don't go around bragging *that you must have done something amazing.*

"God infused our lifeless souls with life." Share what God is speaking to you in this moment. Write a prayer of thanksgiving for what God has done for you.

Elohim created you in His image. He wants you to discover who you are in Him, recognize all the treasures He has bestowed upon you, and live in the fullness of it all!

We continually compare ourselves to others. And because of that comparison, we often believe the lie that we don't measure up. We look in the mirror and criticize, sometimes even detest, the reflection we see. And what we see in that reflection fully depends upon what fills our hearts: biblical truth or the world's lies.

Elohim longs for us to see ourselves as His beautiful creation. The world creates an unrealistic and false image of beauty. Scripture testifies to the accurate image of beauty. God alone is the Author of Life. He alone handcrafted each one of us. And He alone knows the wonderful plans He has for us. Jeremiah 29:11 says they are plans "to prosper you and not to harm you, plans to give you hope and a future" (NIV).

The world creates an unrealistic and false image of beauty. Scripture testifies to the accurate image of beauty.

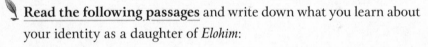

Read Song of Songs 4:7. Write out the verse in the space provided.

Elohim, the Creator of the universe, the One who hung the sun, moon, and stars, formed and shaped *you* and calls *you* beautiful. He created you perfectly for the plans He has for you. You are His handiwork; precious, beautiful, and valuable in His sight.

Apply It

Being made in the image of God means we have within us the capacity to know God intimately and deeply. The moment God seals us with His Spirit, this knowledge becomes a reality as the Spirit quickens us to new life in Christ. We gain the ability to know the deep things of God, to experience His presence, to recognize His voice, to gain His peace, to live in His joy, and to know His love. Friend, you truly are His masterpiece. He loves you deeply and desires that you know Him more and more every day.

Read the following passages and write down what you learn about your identity as a daughter of *Elohim:*

1. Galatians 2:20

2. Ephesians 1:4

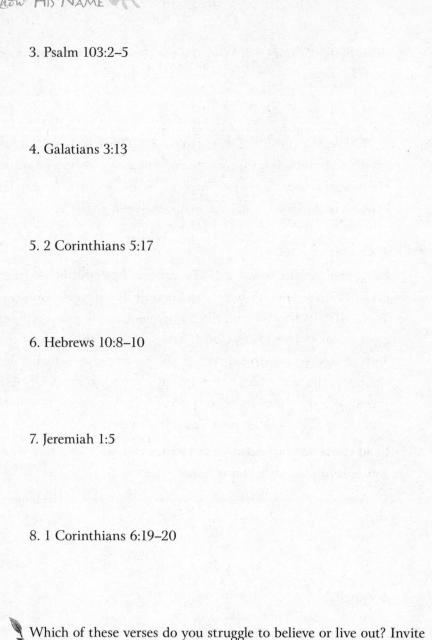

3. Psalm 103:2–5

4. Galatians 3:13

5. 2 Corinthians 5:17

6. Hebrews 10:8–10

7. Jeremiah 1:5

8. 1 Corinthians 6:19–20

Which of these verses do you struggle to believe or live out? Invite God to bring these verses alive in your heart and transform the reflection you see in the mirror so that you will believe them and walk confidently in who you are in Him.

If you're struggling to believe that you are everything that God says you are, or even if you're living with complete confidence in the fact that you're God's precious and dearly loved daughter, I encourage you to pray this prayer with me today.

Elohim, thank You for creating me in Your image and that I am fearfully and wonderfully made. In You, I am forgiven and redeemed and a new creation. Help me discover the woman You created me to be. Give me eyes to see myself as You see me. Father, thank You that I am holy and set apart for Your purposes. Open my eyes to see my true beauty, a beauty that reflects Your heart, Your character, Your strength, and Your dignity. Plant Your truths deep in my heart. Empower me to influence the culture around me. Protect me from being deceived by its lies and temptations. Fill me with Your Holy Spirit and bless me all the days of my life. I ask all this in the name of Your Son, Jesus. Amen.

Part Five:
Jesus

> **Memory Verse:** In the beginning, God created *everything*: the heavens *above* and the *earth below. Here's what happened.*
>
> —Genesis 1:1

Okay, time for a field trip. I'm taking you on a Scripture excavation! We are about to dig deep as we shift from focusing the eyes of our hearts on God and turn them to Jesus.

To do this, let's first revisit Genesis 1:26. God said, "Let *us* make man in *our* image, after our likeness." With these words, God revealed that He has always existed as more than one person. In fact, we learn later in Scripture that He exists as three persons, yet He is one God. But how can God be three persons yet one God?

The church calls this the doctrine of the Trinity. God eternally exists as three persons: Father, Son, and Holy Spirit, and each person is fully God, yet there is only one God.[14] Though Scripture never expressly uses the term *Trinity*, we find its essence in many places, especially in the New Testament. In Matthew 3:16–17, we witness all three persons of the Trinity present and active.

Read Matthew 3:16–17. Write this passage in the space provided.

What role does each person of the Trinity play here?

Matthew returns to the Trinity at the end of his gospel in Jesus' last words to His disciples: "Therefore go and make disciples of all nations, baptizing them in the name of the Father and of the Son and of the Holy Spirit" (Matthew 28:19 NIV).

Read 1 Corinthians 12:4–6; 2 Corinthians 13:14; Ephesians 4:4–6; and 1 Peter 1:2. Share what these verses teach about the roles of each person of the Trinity.

Digging Deeper

In Part One, we learned that God the Father initiated the act of creation. But Genesis 1:26 clearly states that God did not create alone; the concept of the Trinity is essential to today's message.

Read John 1:3; 1 Corinthians 8:6; and Colossians 1:16. What do you learn in these verses?

Just as God has always been, Jesus has always been.

Centuries after creation, John wrote: "In the beginning was the Word, and the Word was with God, and the Word was God. He was with God in the beginning. Through him all things were made; without him nothing was made that has been made" (John

1:1–3 NIV). Just as God has always been, Jesus has always been. They both existed "in the beginning." Before Jesus came into our world in human form, He existed with God the Father. The Nicene Creed, a famous statement of faith formulated by the church in AD 325[15] states:

> I believe in one God the Father Almighty, Maker of heaven and earth, and of all things visible and invisible. And in one Lord Jesus Christ, the only-begotten Son of God, begotten of the Father before all worlds, God of God, Light of Light, Very God of Very God, begotten, not made, being of one substance with the Father by whom all things were made ...

Jesus not only existed with the Father but also created with the Father.

Read Psalm 33:6. Describe how God created the heavens.

Jesus cocreated our universe with His Father. John 1:3 goes even further and says "without him nothing was made that has been made." Jesus joined His Father to hang the stars, fill the seas, sculpt the mountains, mark the seasons, and knit together each and every creature that crawls and walks on the face of the earth. Colossians 1:15–17 says, "The Son is the image of the invisible God, the firstborn over all creation. For in him all things were created: things in heaven and on earth, visible and invisible, whether thrones or powers or rulers or authorities; all things have been created through him and for him. He is before all things, and in him all things hold together" (NIV).

Paul's words in Colossians affirm John's teaching. Jesus is the "image" of the invisible God, meaning "the exact representation and revelation" of God.[16] John 1:18 says, "God, unseen until now, is revealed in the Voice, God's only Son, *straight* from the Father's heart." And Hebrews 1:3 says, "This is the One who—imprinted with God's image, shimmering His glory—sustains all that exists through the power of His Word ..." In Jesus, God is perfectly revealed in human form. John 14:9 says, "If you have seen me, you have seen the Father." While nature reveals the existence, creative power, wisdom, and glory of God, Jesus reveals the very essence of God.

Next, in Colossians 1:15, Paul described Jesus as God's "first-born." The term as used here does not refer to actual birth order, like the first born of many children. Rather, the word refers to Jesus' status. God has given His Son positional authority.

This conveys two important facts about Christ. First, He preceded all of creation. Second, He is sovereign over all creation. Paul used this word because his audience, composed of mostly Hebrew Christians, was familiar with the Old Testament significance of the firstborn. A Jewish firstborn child had not only the priority of birth but also the honor and superiority that went with it.

Paul continued in verse 16, saying, "in him all things were created." He created everything in heaven and on earth, visible and invisible.

Read Matthew 8:26 and Matthew 14:13–21. How do these stories speak to the truths that Paul taught concerning Jesus?

And Jesus, like God, is eternal. He was, is, and always will be. Jesus asserted His eternity in John 8. Here we read of a crowd of angry Jews, many of them Pharisees, challenging the claims Jesus made about Himself. Jesus asked if any of them could prove Him guilty of sin. Since they had no answer, they accused Him of being a Samaritan and demon-possessed. They harbored deep hatred and resentment for Jesus and desired nothing more than to kill Him. And they had no idea that He was about to go to the cross for them, to give His life for theirs. In answer to their accusations about His identity, Jesus stood boldly before the assembly and answered them with these words in John 8:58, "Very truly I tell you ... before Abraham was born, I am!" (NIV).

Read Exodus 3:14. Why are Jesus' words here significant?

Notice that Jesus did not say, "Before Abraham was, I *was*." He said, "Before Abraham was, I *am*." He was telling them that He is Jehovah, the I AM, *Elohim*. Make no mistake. His audience knew precisely what Jesus was claiming, because in the very next verse they took up stones to kill Him for blasphemy!

Read Revelation 22:13. What does Jesus call Himself?

Read Revelation 1:8. What does the Lord God call Himself?

This is not the only place we see Jesus talking about who He is in relation to creation and time. Alpha and Omega are the first and last letters of the Greek alphabet, the language in which most of the New Testament was written. God defines Himself as the beginning and the end (Revelation 1:8). He sovereignly rules over all of human history. Jesus applied these same words to Himself in

Revelation 22:13, constituting a strong claim to equal deity with God the Father. Christ is before all creation and will continue to exist after our universe is destroyed. He, like God the Father, is the Eternal One!

Before we close our chapter, let's examine one more word from Peter about Jesus. "He was chosen before the creation of the world, but was revealed in these last times for your sake" (1 Peter 1:20 NIV). Now read this same verse in The Voice: "God determined to send Him before the world began, but He came *into the world* in these last days for your sake. Through Him, you've been brought to trust in God, who raised Him from the dead and glorified Him for the very reason that your faith and hope are in Him" (1 Peter 1:20–21).

Peter's words in Acts 2:23 also confirm that Jesus' coming to earth and what happened to Him while He was here were part of God's grand plan: "this man, *Jesus*, who came into your hands by God's sure plan and advanced knowledge ..." Before time began, both God the Father and God the Son knew that this would be Jesus' mission. Even before they created the world, God designated His Son to be our Savior and Redeemer!

Jesus is

... the visible expression of the invisible God.

... the living expression of His Father's heart.

... the written expression of His Father's mind.

... the creative expression of His Father's hand.

... the perfect expression of His Father's will.

So doesn't it only make sense that if we want to know more about *Elohim*, we must get to know more about His Son? Throughout the rest of our journey together, we will do just that.

>> Apply It

Creation leads us to the Creator. The sheer breadth of the heavens and the vast expanse of the earth point to an all-powerful Creator. The awe-inspiring heights jutting forth from the Colorado Rocky Mountains and the breathtaking palette painted across an Ocean Isle Beach sunset point to a personal and intimate God. A God who says, "Look, I am here!" God didn't have to create such wonders; He chose to create them. He built them into our world. As gifts. As signs. As wonders to point us to His majesty and His glory. To point us to *Elohim*.

On earth, *Elohim* unveils Himself bit by bit. But one day we will gaze into the eyes of our Creator. It will no longer be a reflection of His glory that we see, like the breathtaking flight of the eagle or the vibrant colors of a sunset. It will be our Great God Himself. The Creator of heaven and earth. It will be *Elohim* in the fullness of all His glory.

> *On earth, Elohim unveils Himself bit by bit. But one day we will gaze into the eyes of our Creator.*

No more will we experience God through His created things. Such things will no longer satisfy; they will no longer fill us with awe and wonder. *He will.*

I cannot wait for that day! What about you?

But until that glorious day when we meet our Father in heaven, the One who is the Author of Life, we will have to choose what we believe: either Jesus is who He says He is, or He is not. *What will you choose to believe?*

My prayer is that you will choose to believe Jesus' words that He is the great I AM, Jehovah God, *Elohim*.

Here are two final questions for this section. Take time to prayerfully answer them based on what you have learned from God's Word and what God has spoken into your heart throughout your time with Him.

Who is *Elohim*?

What does this mean for my life?

Prayer:

You are Elohim, who made everything out of nothing, created order out of chaos, gave birth to all of nature, and called it good. Enable me to comprehend the vastness of Your glory and learn to live my life in a way that forever magnifies Your holy name.

Optional Video Study

Use the space below to note anything that stands out to you from the video teaching. You may also choose to take notes on a separate sheet of paper.

Use the following questions as a guide for group discussion:

What one thing stood out to you most in this chapter?

How can you apply the name of God you studied this week to your own life and current situation?

Take a few moments to review this week's memory verse together. What does this verse mean to you personally?

Could you relate to any of the people or situations from the Bible that you studied this week? If so, how?

CHAPTER TWO

El Roi: The One Who Sees You

Prayer:

Heavenly Father, El Roi, the God Who Sees, thank You that I am never alone, that there is no place I can go where You will not be with me. Thank You that when I stray, You seek; when I am lost, You find; when I am hurt, You heal; when I am empty, You fill; when I am hungry, You feed; when I fail, You restore. I know You are with me all the time. Enable me to sense Your presence in the midst of my everyday life. Manifest Yourself to me as You did to Hagar, to Moses, and to Elijah. Open the eyes of my heart to receive abundant wisdom and knowledge as I learn another of Your magnificent names. I ask all this in the name of Your Son, Jesus Christ my Lord, the Good Shepherd. Amen.

Part One:
Abram, Sarai, and Hagar

> **Memory Verse:** She gave this name to the LORD who spoke to her: "You are the God who sees me."
>
> —Genesis 16:13a (NIV)

To begin this part of our study, we'll return to Genesis to unearth another wonderful name of God. But this time we will unpack His name through the lens of a profoundly dysfunctional family.

Read Genesis 16.

Let's get familiar with Abram (Abraham's name before God renamed him) and his family before we dig into our story. At age seventy-five, God called Abram to leave his country, his people, and all that he knew to go to an unknown land that God would show him. Abram obeyed and took his family with him. Both before he left, and along the journey, God made great promises to Abram.

When Abram turned ninety, God promised Abram and Sarai (Sarah's name before God renamed her) a son. God took Abram outside and said, "Look up at the stars, and try to count them all if you can. *There are too many to count!* Your descendants will be as *many* as the stars" (Genesis 15:5).

But for years, Sarai failed to get pregnant. In his head, Abram knew God would be faithful because He had been faithful in the past. But the waiting was hard. Can you relate? Have you ever waited on God? The spirit is willing, but the flesh is weak! Abram and Sarai weren't getting any younger.

When Sarai could not take the waiting any longer, she took matters into her own hands. She purposed in her heart to hurry God's plan, to accomplish through human effort what she believed God was not doing on His own.

How many times have we done the same thing? We long for something, but it doesn't happen on our timetable. We grow impatient and manipulate circumstances to make it happen.

> Sarai purposed in her heart to hurry God's plan, to accomplish through human effort what she believed God was not doing on His own. How many times have we done the same thing?

Digging Deeper

Reread Genesis 16:1–4.

Sarai's words to her husband in Genesis 16:2 revealed the bitterness in her heart: "You can see that the Eternal One has still not allowed me to have any children. Why don't you sleep with my servant girl? Maybe I could *use her as a surrogate and* have a child through her!" God hadn't followed through with His promise, so Sarai conjured up a scheme to have a baby sooner rather than later.

Sarai told Abram to sleep with her servant girl, Hagar. And since Hagar was just a slave girl and this was a familiar ancient custom, Sarai probably reasoned that it was no big deal to use the young girl this way.

How did Abram, God's chosen one, respond to Sarai's request?

Knowing the promise God had made to him, why do you think Abram didn't stand up to Sarai and say no to her request?

Sadly, Abram and Sarai lost sight of God's promises. They abandoned the way of faith and chose their own way instead. Their decision opened the door to much misery. Because they believed themselves wiser than God, their family would never be the same again.

Has there been a time in your life where you lost sight of God's promises? Reflect on what it felt like during that time and what happened.

In just these few short verses, we have learned a monumental life lesson. Failing to trust God at His Word, making decisions in the heat of the moment, and allowing ourselves to be led by self and not by God's Spirit, will lead to life-altering consequences we can never take back. Although our God is a God of grace, the pain that results from our impatience can have lingering repercussions, some that last a lifetime. And in Sarai's case, the consequence of her impatience was that Hagar became pregnant.

Failing to trust God at His Word, making decisions in the heat of the moment, and allowing ourselves to be led by self and not by God's Spirit, will lead to life-altering consequences we can never take back.

Reread Genesis 16:5–6. How did Sarai respond to Abram and Hagar after she learned Hagar was pregnant?

The women grew to despise each other as Abram's child grew within Hagar's belly. Sarai mistreated Hagar terribly. To escape her cruelty, Hagar fled. How desperate she must have felt—pregnant, alone, and rejected for doing what she was told to do.

What do you think of Sarai's actions? Abram's? Hagar's?

Thankfully, Scripture reveals a ray of hope in Genesis 16:7–13.

Reread Genesis 16:7–13.

What emotions does this story elicit in you?

Who found Hagar in Genesis 16:7?

Who do you think the angel of the Lord was?

This is the first of many references to "the angel of the LORD" in the Old Testament. Most scholars believe the angel to be a "Christophany," a preincarnate appearance of Christ (Christ coming to earth before He came as a baby in the New Testament). Grasp the implication of these words. In the midst of her despair, Hagar encountered Jesus! The Son of God left His rightful place in heaven, cloaked Himself in a temporary body, and came down to minister to this desperate, rejected servant girl. In the midst of Hagar's deepest grief, He found her. He shined the light of His hope into the darkness suffocating Hagar's heart.

This is our God! What a beautiful revelation of God's amazing grace and unconditional love!

And did you notice that in Genesis 16:8, the angel of the Lord called her by name. He not only called her by name but also defined who she was. He called her "servant of Sarai." He identified her in this way to prepare her heart for the words He was about to speak.

What two questions did the angel of the Lord ask Hagar?

How did she answer?

The angel gave Hagar two declarations: "go back ... *and change your attitude.* Be respectful and listen to her instructions" (Genesis 16:9). What hard words these must have been for her to receive. It was probably the last thing she wanted, to go back to the woman who had caused her so much grief and submit to her authority. But the reality was, Hagar was a servant and had disrespected Abram and Sarai by running away. And in so doing, she risked the life of her unborn child.

I don't know about you, but submission is sometimes difficult for me—so very difficult, especially when I feel I have been wronged. But God knows that in most cases, submission is in our best interest.

Then the angel of the Lord gave Hagar a promise in Genesis 16:10. He first promised Hagar that He would increase her descendants so much that they would be too numerous to count.

To whom does God make this same promise in Genesis 17:20?

Although Hagar's child would not share in the blessings of the covenant God made with Abram, he would still enjoy blessings from God since he was Abram's son.

Read Genesis 25:12–18. What did God promise?

Returning to Genesis 16:11, the angel of the Lord then revealed to Hagar that she would have a son and that she was to name the boy Ishmael.

What reason did the angel of the Lord give for that specific name?

Her son's name commemorated God's intervention in her time of desperate need. *Ishmael* means "God hears." God heard the cry of Hagar's heart and was faithful to respond. And because our God is the same yesterday, today, and forever, He is still faithful today and hears the cries of our hearts as well (Hebrews 13:8).

Hagar expressed her gratitude by giving God a special name: "El Roi" (16:13 NIV).

What words did Hagar speak immediately after she gave this name to God in verse 13?

She celebrated the fact that God saw her alone in the wilderness and did not abandon her. He rescued her and gave her hope and direction. She then marked the spot of her encounter with *El Roi* by naming it "Beer Lahai Roi" which means *"Well of the Living One who watches over me"* (Genesis 16:14).

The angel of the Lord revealed one more thing about Hagar's son in Genesis 16:12.

Read this verse. What did God reveal?

God described Ishmael as a "wild and rowdy man." The NIV uses the words *a wild donkey*, probably referring to an onager, a wild donkey that roamed the desert land. Ishmael would be a hated man, living "in hostility toward all his brothers" (Genesis 16:12 NIV). So although, like Isaac, Ishmael would become the father of a great tribe, his descendants would be a wild, hostile people living in the Arabian Desert—not God's chosen ones.

Read Genesis 25:12–18. What do you learn about Ishmael and his descendants?

These verses reveal the fulfillment of the promises made to Hagar and Abram concerning their son (Genesis 16:10, 12; 17:20). Ishmael's descendants would not be the promised seed of Abraham. They would forever live as bitter enemies of God's people.

One interesting note about the Ishmaelites is found still later in Genesis.

Read Genesis 37:12–28. What do you learn about the Ishmaelites?

Apply It

Aren't you grateful that God didn't create our world and then walk away to leave us on our own? I sure am. Our God is a personal God; He is always here with us. He sees us and He knows each and every detail of our lives.

No matter how difficult our circumstances, we never solve life's problems by running away. Hagar's wilderness experience brought her face-to-face with the living God and taught her (and us) some important truths:

No matter how difficult our circumstances, we never solve life's problems by running away.

- God will find us.

- God knows us by name.

- God sees us and hears our cries.

- God is concerned about our burdens and our cares.

- God knows our future.

Are you, like Hagar, in a place of wilderness today? What struggles are you facing? Take a moment to reflect on your own life and to write down any areas in which you may be struggling. Know that you are not there alone. God hears you and sees you! Take what you have learned from Hagar's story and apply it to your circumstances. Allow *El Roi* to begin a work in you.

Now write down some steps of obedience you can take to move out of your wilderness into a place of hope.

Part Two:
The Good Shepherd

> **Memory Verse:** She gave this name to the LORD who
> spoke to her: "You are the God who sees me."
>
> —Genesis 16:13a (NIV)

We find *El Roi* throughout the pages of Scripture. Today we find
Him in one of the best known and most beloved passages, Psalm 23.
Maybe this passage is very familiar to you. Or, perhaps you're read-
ing it for the very first time. Either way, I encourage you to invite
God to open your heart to receive it in a fresh way.

Read Psalm 23.

> The Eternal is my shepherd, He cares for me always.
> He provides me rest in rich, green fields beside streams of
>   refreshing water.
>   *He soothes my fears;*
> He makes me whole again, steering me *off worn, hard paths*
>   to roads where *truth and* righteousness echo His name.
>
> Even in the *unending* shadows of death's darkness, I am not
>   overcome by fear.
> Because You are with me *in those dark moments*, near with Your
>   protection and guidance,
>   I am comforted.
>
> You spread out a table before me,
>   *provisions* in the midst of *attack from* my enemies;
> *You care for all my needs*, anointing my head with *soothing, fragrant*
>   oil, filling my cup again and again with *Your grace.*
> Certainly Your faithful protection and loving provision will
>   pursue me where I go, always, everywhere.
> I will always be with the Eternal, in Your house forever.

Through the words of this psalm, David not only invited us into the life of an Old Testament shepherd but also revealed in a new way the character of our God. As David pondered how he cared for his sheep, the Lord flooded his heart with the overwhelming conviction that God cares for His people in the same way.

In this passage, David paints a lovely portrait of God our Shepherd. A shepherd leads, provides for, and protects his flock. He knows each sheep by name and values each one more than his own life. He will risk injury and even his life to find a stray sheep and bring it back to the flock. Listen to David's own words as he spoke to King Saul about Goliath:

> I work as a shepherd for my father. Whenever a lion or a bear has come and attacked one of my lambs, I have gone after it and struck it down to rescue the lamb from the predator's mouth; if it turned to attack me, I would take it by the chin, beat it, and kill it. I have killed both a lion and a bear; and as your servant I will kill this uncircumcised Philistine, too, since he has dared to taunt the armies of the living God. (1 Samuel 17:34–36)

Reread Psalm 23 in your own Bible.

In your own words, according to Psalm 23, what does a shepherd do for his sheep?

Digging Deeper

David followed in the footsteps of many of the great men of God in the Old Testament. Before being called by God, Abraham, Isaac, Jacob, and Moses all served as shepherds. God surely revered the heart of a shepherd, and saw something valuable and useful in this humble occupation.

Let's look at the duties of a shepherd. A good shepherd faithfully tends his sheep; finds fresh pastures to graze; clears the pasture of rocks and stones; levels the ground; and stands guard while the sheep eat. He cares for the weak and doctors the wounded. He provides water to quench their thirst. At night, he leads them home to ensure their safety. His protective eye is always upon them. As he considered these duties and his personal experiences as a shepherd, David concluded that the Lord watched over him in the same way he watched over his sheep.

Read Psalm 23:1. When the Lord is our shepherd, what do we lack?

Think about your own life. Is there something you feel you lack (hope, joy, finances, confidence, etc.)? If you answered yes, what do you think is behind that sense of "lacking"?

Now let's walk through the blessings David received from his Good Shepherd.

First Blessing: Nourishment

In Psalm 23:2, David wrote that God made him lie down in "rich green fields." In Hebrew, *green* translates "sprout, tender grass"[1]; and *fields*, as used here, means "a pleasant place."[2] A shepherd takes his sheep to pleasant places where they can receive nourishment and rest. They feel content and secure as they eat and sleep because their shepherd has led them and is watching over them.

Similarly, the first blessing David experienced with the Lord as his Shepherd was nourishment—spiritual nourishment. Just as David knew what his sheep needed, so *El Roi* knows what we need.

> *Just as David knew what his sheep needed, so El Roi knows what we need.*

Friend, remember *El Roi* is also *Elohim*, our Creator. He knows us inside and out. Nothing is hidden. Our every hurt, doubt, fear, and need is on display before Him. So when our Creator *El Roi* "sees" our need, He will come to us, meet with us, feed us, refresh us, and renew us, just as He did Hagar.

Who or what do you look to in times of stress, anxiety, and need (food, friends, alcohol, drugs, shopping, or God)? How has this response worked for you?

Read Psalm 139:7–12. How does this passage speak to what we have learned about *El Roi*? How does this comfort you in your own circumstances?

Second Blessing: Restoration

Just as David led his sheep to quiet waters for refreshment and restoration, *El Roi* does the same for us. We live in a world where nothing ever stops. News twenty-four hours a day. Shopping twenty-four hours a day. Television twenty-four hours a day. Combine this with twenty-four-hour-a-day social media, and we have access to most anything we want, any time we want it.

That also means that unless we intentionally create time for renewal and refreshment, it will not happen. Schedules exhaust us. Life's fast pace drains us. Coworkers annoy us. Husbands aggravate us. And children just plain wear us out. Even our "fellow sheep," our brothers and sisters in Christ, try us to our limits at times! How do we escape this merry-go-round life?

Unless we intentionally create time for renewal and refreshment, it will not happen.

El Roi is our escape. He sees our weariness and longs to meet with us. He leads us to Himself—to His living water. Sure, we can curl up for a nap. We can take a day off. We can schedule a week-long vacation once a year. But it's not enough. We need time for spiritual restoration and revival. We need to literally take time to "be still." It's only when we decide to rest that God is able to lead us beside quiet waters and refresh our souls.

But we have to be willing to be led. It's in that place of stillness and quiet that we experience the increased presence of the Lord—the fullness of His love, His peace, His joy, and His patience.

Psalm 23:3 says our Shepherd will soothe or refresh our souls. What does David mean when he refers to our "soul"? My favorite biblical definition of *soul*, from Psalm 103, uses the Hebrew word *nephesh*, defined as "our entire being."[3] God causes us to rest and leads us beside still waters because He knows how much we need to rest physically, spiritually, and emotionally.

Apply It

Maybe you're a mama right in the midst of diaper changes, middle-of-the-night feedings, and preschool playdates. Or, you might be working long hours and constantly traveling across the country for business meetings. You might even be an empty nester trying to find your new "normal" now that the children have left home. Whatever your stage of life, I encourage you to let the Good Shepherd lead you to places of rest, to renew your soul, to fill you with His sweet presence. He sees you and He knows what you need.

Examine your day-to-day schedule. Does it allow time for God to "make you lie down in green pastures" and "lead you beside quiet waters"? If not, what in your schedule needs to change to allow time for God to do this?

What practical steps could you take that would allow you to have more time to be led by God to places of quietness, stillness, and rest? Write down a few things you think God might be able to do in your life if you spent some time just resting and being quiet in His presence.

Part Three:
Paths of Our Good Shepherd

> **Memory Verse:** She gave this name to the LORD who spoke to her: "You are the God who sees me."
>
> —Genesis 16:13a (NIV)

Let's continue our journey through Psalm 23 as we walk through more of the blessings David received from his Good Shepherd.

Read Psalm 23:3b–4. In the space provided write out these verses in your own words.

Third Blessing: Paths of Righteousness

David writes that our Good Shepherd steers us off "worn, hard paths" and leads us to "roads where truth and righteousness echo His name." The King James Version says He leads us down "paths of righteousness" and the NIV says "right paths."

Take a few minutes to write down some characteristics of "right" and "wrong" paths. On what path do you find yourself most often and why? (If you're like me, you may find yourself on both paths, depending on the day or the circumstances.)

🖋 In your own words, define what David means by "roads where truth and righteousness echo His name."

A good shepherd leads his sheep. Because David had traversed his father's land for years and was familiar with every inch of it, he knew the best, safest ways to lead his sheep. So he faithfully led them along those safe, familiar paths.

It's the same for us. Jeremiah 29:11 tells us that God knows the plans He has for us, and He knows the best way to accomplish those plans. So we can trust He will lead us down the paths best suited for that plan. And as long as we stay close to His heart, He will lead us step by step.

> *God knows the plans He has for us, and He knows the best way to accomplish those plans. So we can trust He will lead us down the paths best suited for that plan.*

Did you notice *why* God leads us along right paths? The Bible says, "for his name's sake." He leads in accordance with all His name represents. Goodness. Holiness. Faithfulness. Unconditional love, to name a few. Even when we don't understand the path God chooses for us, we can trust it is the "right path" because we trust His name and the character that His name represents.

Pondering this truth brings to mind Mary, the mother of Jesus. In one moment in time, this ordinary girl who lived an ordinary life came face-to-face with an extraordinary God. God's eyes had searched the whole earth to find a young woman to be the mother of His Son. When His search stopped in the little town of Nazareth, He sent the angel Gabriel to tell Mary the good news. Luke tells us that Gabriel's greeting "greatly troubled" Mary (Luke 1:29 NIV). Gabriel, sensing the fear welling up within her, quieted her heart with these words: "Mary, don't be afraid. You have found favor with God. Listen, you are going to become pregnant. You will have a son, and you must name Him 'Savior,' *or* Jesus" (Luke 1:30–31).

Can you imagine what ran through Mary's mind on hearing this news? Scripture tells us she was a virgin. Everyone knew she was a virgin. But as her belly grew, enveloping the Christ child, what would people think? What would they say? More importantly, what would Joseph, the man to whom she was betrothed, say? I'm sure this is not the "path" Mary thought her life would take. Yet it was the "right path" down which God was going to lead her.

Read Luke 1:34–38. What was Mary's response to the path God had chosen for her?

How would you respond if God did something similar in your life, calling you to walk a path you didn't expect?

Why do you think Mary was able to so quickly put aside her doubts about this surprising proclamation and all it would entail and surrender her will to God's?

It's so important that we know *El Roi* intimately—His goodness, His faithfulness, and His unconditional love. It's only when we know Him this way that we can be assured that every path down which He leads us will be for our good, even when we cannot see it with our eyes or feel it in our hearts.

Reread Psalm 23:4.

Fourth Blessing: Protection

As our family gathered around my father-in-law in his hospital room just days before he went to be with Jesus, David's words from Psalm 23:4 comforted my grieving soul: "Even in the *unending* shadows of death's darkness, I am not overcome by fear. Because You are with me *in those dark moments,* near with Your protection and guidance, I am comforted."

The NIV says, "Even though I walk through the darkest valley," and the King James Version says, "Yea, though I walk through the valley of the shadow of death." David's words do not necessarily mean *literal* death; they also refer to the dark, lonely, fearful places in which we sometimes find ourselves. But no matter how dark the darkest place is, David writes that we need not be afraid because *El Roi* is with us, watching over us.

David knew the dark places all too well. Saul, the first king of Israel, despised David and plotted to kill him, no matter the cost. He hunted David like an animal, forcing him to flee into the wilderness. David lived, often alone and isolated, in fear and desperation for years. But he was not alone. Other great men of God—Moses, Elijah, the prophets, Stephen, Peter, Paul, and even Jesus Himself— walked through the darkest of valleys and found the comfort and safety of *El Roi* in the midst of them.

Read Romans 8:35–38. How does this New Testament passage speak to this truth?

We hear this passage quoted often during times of suffering, but do we remember the trials and sufferings of the one who wrote these verses? These power-packed words were penned by Paul, a man who endured greater adversity than we could ever imagine. Paul writes these words to encourage us.

Read 2 Corinthians 11:21–33.

Although it's very unlikely that we'll ever experience suffering as deep as Paul's, we do at times experience seemingly unbearable trials. Suffering is not new to God's people. It has always been a part of God's story. But we must never forget that no matter how great or small, short or enduring, the strain of suffering, it will never, ever separate us from *El Roi*. In fact, when seen through the lens of God's truth and His character, suffering actually moves us closer to the heart of God. It has divine purpose. Our suffering works in and through us to conform us to the image of God's Son and make us more like Him.

No matter how great or small, short or enduring, the strain of suffering, it will never, ever separate us from El Roi.

In the midst of his suffering, David wrote "your rod and your staff, they comfort me" (Psalm 23:4 NIV). The rod and staff are tools of the shepherd's trade. The shepherd wielded the rod to protect his sheep by driving off wild animals; he used the staff to guide the flock and lift them back on the path if they fell. Clearly, the rod and staff in the hands of God gave David comfort and should give us assurance as well.

God never slumbers. He never takes a catnap. His eyes are always upon His kingdom. We see another beautiful illustration of this truth just before God's people crossed the Jordan River into the Promised Land. As Moses commissioned their new leader, Joshua, he spoke these words: "Be strong and brave! You're going to lead these people into the land the Eternal One promised their ancestors He'd give them … And He will be leading you. He'll be with you, and He'll never fail you or abandon you. So don't be afraid!" (Deuteronomy 31:7–8).

Apply It

David, the shepherd, led his sheep. He knew his sheep intimately and called them by name. They followed him because they recognized his voice. They followed his voice and his voice alone. David never abandoned his sheep. If one wandered off, he searched far and wide to find it. When he found that little sheep, he laid it across his shoulders and carried it home to safety. When David said in Psalm 23, "The LORD is my shepherd" (NIV), he likely envisioned God caring for him the way he cared for his own sheep.

And God, *El Roi*, does the same for you, tenderly watching over you. He alone is *your* Shepherd. He knows you and calls you by name. He loves you and will never leave you or forsake you. These are His promises.

If you don't know your Shepherd, I invite you to familiarize yourself with Him. Read His Word so that you may know it. Listen for His voice. As *El Roi* unveils His nature and character to you, He will care for you. He will make you lie down in green pastures. He will restore your soul. He will give you rest. He will remain with you always. He will comfort and protect you.

El Roi is the God who sees you. He is *your* Shepherd.

Reread Psalm 23:4. Think back to some of your own darkest moments. Write down how God worked during that time in your life.

Perhaps you're walking through a dark time now. Use a blank notecard to write down Psalm 23. Hang it somewhere that you will see it often. Rehearse God's promise to never leave you; fill your mind with God's Word, and allow it to bring peace and comfort to you.

Part Four: Elijah

> **Memory Verse:** She gave this name to the LORD who spoke to her: "You are the God who sees me."
>
> —Genesis 16:13a (NIV)

It's time to meet Elijah (his name means "my God is Yahweh"), one of God's most illustrious prophets. He lived in the ninth century BC during the reign of King Ahab, one of Israel's strongest yet most evil kings. Just how evil was King Ahab? First Kings 16:30 says of him, "Ahab (Omri's son) committed evil in the Eternal's eyes. He was more wicked than all *the wicked kings* who lived before him."

Ahab married Jezebel, one of the cruelest and most hated women in Israel. They made quite the pair. Together they forced everyone, including the Israelites, to worship Jezebel's god, Baal. Jezebel persecuted and severely punished anyone who chose to worship the God of Israel over her god. At one point, she ordered the mass killing of all God's prophets and succeeded in killing all but one hundred of them. Still, Elijah stood boldly for God and against Jezebel as idolatry swept through God's land.

Jews, Christians, and Muslims regard Elijah to this day as a great hero because of his tremendous courage during that time.

Let's dig a bit into the life and story of Elijah, whom God called to serve as His prophet during King Ahab's reign. In 1 Kings 17, Elijah warned Ahab of the coming of a great drought. After he issued his prophetic warning, Elijah went into hiding at God's command. The drought came and caused King Ahab so much grief and anguish that he ordered his men to find and capture Elijah. During those years, Elijah lived as a fugitive.

🖋 **Read 1 Kings 17** if you want to know more about Elijah's time on the run.

God then gave Elijah another message for King Ahab and ordered him out of hiding to deliver it. Elijah obeyed, despite the impending danger due to Jezebel's terrifying edict to kill every true prophet of God. When Elijah appeared before Ahab, the King greeted him with these words: "There you are. *I thought I perceived* a troublemaker in Israel" (1 Kings 18:17).

King Ahab didn't know how spot-on he was with those words. Oh, yes, there was a troublemaker in Israel. But it was not Elijah. Israel's troubles were rooted not in Elijah and his prophecy but in the sins of Ahab, his father Omri, and the Israelite people.

Elijah's next steps were bold and courageous. Confident in the power and might of Israel's God, he challenged the 450 prophets of Baal to a showdown on Mount Carmel to determine who prayed more effectively—Elijah, the prophet of God, or the 450 prophets of Baal. Elijah won the contest in a most incredible display of God's power and glory. "When everyone witnessed this *extraordinary power*, they all put their faces to the ground *in fear and awe and wonder* ... [the people cried]: The Eternal One is the True God! The Eternal One is the True God!" (1 Kings 18:39).

🖋 **Read 1 Kings 18:16–39.**

When Elijah commanded those present to seize and slay the prophets of Baal, then and only then did the rain come, ending the years of drought (1 Kings 18:39–46). Even though the drought was over, the news of the slaughter of her prophets enraged Jezebel, and she swore she'd kill Elijah for what he had done.

⟩⟩ Digging Deeper

In 1 Kings 18 we encounter a bold and courageous Elijah.

🖋 **Read 1 Kings 18:45–46.** How would you characterize Elijah after his victory at Mount Carmel?

But then, a strange transformation occurred.

🖋 **Read 1 Kings 19:1–5.** How would you characterize Elijah in this passage?

🖋 What do you think caused this change?

Elijah's confidence crumbled. One threatening message from a vengeful queen dispelled every ounce of his courage. Although God had dramatically demonstrated His power and might through Elijah; although God had exalted Elijah above all other prophets; although Elijah's God showed that He was the one true God of heaven and earth, Elijah's faith suddenly failed him. What happened?

We don't know for certain because Scripture doesn't tell us. Perhaps Elijah thought seeing God's power would turn the hearts of Ahab and Jezebel toward Yahweh and give Elijah favor in their eyes, when it only enraged them instead. Although the text does not tell us directly, it's quite apparent that something shattered Elijah's faith.

Reread 1 Kings 19:4 and write the words Elijah spoke to God below.

Have you ever been there—that place of gloom and despair where nothing makes sense? You can't see or hear God in the midst of the darkness. Defeat overcomes you on every side.

That's where we find Elijah. Even though God had just shown Himself in miraculous ways through Elijah, the prophet concluded that his work was fruitless and his life was no longer worth living. After running for his life and crying out to God to take his life, Scripture says Elijah lay down and fell asleep. He was simply exhausted. Goodness! Let's hang out there for a second. How many of us have been stuck there before—weak in our faith, confidence lost, doubting our call, simply exhausted?

I have good news for you! God did not abandon Elijah because he lost his confidence, because he was weak and doubting his call. God did not leave Elijah there alone in the wilderness—and He won't leave you there either.

God did not abandon Elijah because he lost his confidence, because he was weak and doubting his call. God did not leave Elijah there alone in the wilderness—and He won't leave you there either.

What lessons can we glean from Elijah's story? First, when we walk through a trying time, whether good or bad, we have immediate physical needs that need to be satisfied—most especially rest and nourishment. How precious it is to know that God sees these needs and provides for them.

Read 1 Kings 19:5–9a. What did God do for Elijah?

God provided for his beloved Elijah. Verse 5 tells us that when Elijah fell asleep, an angel came, touched him, and instructed him: "Get up, and eat." In His mercy, the Lord lovingly and graciously sent an angel to feed and nourish Elijah. If we find ourselves in despair or deep depression, we need to take heed of God's lesson taught here: Get rest and eat well. Did you notice how God provided food immediately, before He even spoke a single word to Elijah?

After God fed him, Elijah fell back asleep. The angel of the Lord came back, awakened him again, and told him to eat, so he obeyed. Through rest and nourishment, God readied Elijah for the next leg of his journey.

Read 1 Kings 19:9. How long did Elijah travel? Name two other men of God who were sustained by the Lord for the same amount of time. (See Exodus 24:18; 34:28; Matthew 4:2, 11.)

After traveling, where did Elijah end up and what happened there? (See 1 Kings 19:9–10.)

This reminds me of Genesis 3:9 when the Lord asked Adam and Eve, "Where are you?" Obviously, the Lord knew where they were. *El Roi* never takes His eyes off of His children. So when He asked Elijah what he was doing in the cave, God already knew. He wanted Elijah to acknowledge what was going on in his heart and confess it because it was his heart that needed healing.

Elijah's response exposed his prideful preoccupation with his own self-importance: "*I* have been very zealous for the Lord God Almighty" (1 Kings 19:10 NIV, emphasis added). His response could also reveal that, since he was the only prophet left, perhaps he felt indispensable to God: "The Israelites have rejected your covenant, torn down your altars, and put your prophets to death … *I* am the only one left" (verse 10 NIV, emphasis added).

Elijah fixed his thoughts on the physical, what he could see and hear—on his enemies and their power, rather than on God and His power. He ignored God's sovereignty and the fact that God needed no one to do His work for Him. It's as if Elijah believed that the work the Lord had begun centuries before had now come to nothing.

God *chooses* us to be instruments in His hand to do His work. He allows us to be a part of His grand plans on this earth, but He depends on no one.

God chooses us to be instruments in His hand to do His work. He allows us to be a part of His grand plans on this earth, but He depends on no one.

Finally, Elijah's words reveal how lonely and scared he felt since he was one of the few prophets still living. We can almost hear the fear and self-pity in his trembling words: "now they are trying to kill me too" (1 Kings 19:10 NIV). This is what my friend calls "stinkin' thinkin'"! Elijah forgot one very important truth from 1 Samuel 17:47: "All those gathered here will know that it is not by sword or spear that the LORD saves; for the battle is the LORD's, and he will give all of you into our hands" (NIV). The battle is never dependent upon human strength; it's always dependent upon God.

As we review Elijah's story, we discover *El Roi* is a God of order. First, *El Roi*, the God Who Sees, sought Elijah out.

Read Psalm 103:8–18. How does this psalm speak to the character of God as exhibited through Elijah's story?

Next, before God dealt with Elijah's spiritual condition, He addressed the prophet's basic physical needs. He rejuvenated him physically with rest and nourishment. Elijah could not take the next steps God needed him to take without regaining physical and emotional strength.

Then, *El Roi* cut straight to the "heart of the matter," but not by instructions or commands. God asked a simple question that caused Elijah to examine his heart, to ponder what he was doing and why. God wanted Elijah to process his emotions *and* his actions.

Read 1 Kings 19:11–14. What happened next?

What question did God ask Elijah again in verse 13b? Why do you think God asked that question again?

What was Elijah's answer?

Elijah did not respond in the way God had hoped. He still looked at his circumstances through the lens of fear and self-pity. God had to do something significant to touch Elijah's heart and change his perspective.

What is the significance of God speaking, not through the powerful forces of nature, but through a whisper?

God often used common elements such as earthquake, wind, and fire to dramatically and decisively judge evil. Sometimes He even appeared in the elements themselves (the burning bush, the pillar of fire). Elijah expected God to do it again at Mount Carmel, but instead he found himself on the run.

Elijah's deliverance from his sense of failure, his lack of self-worth, and his depression did not come until he learned that God works in many ways, not just in the "mighty" acts and the miracles. Sometimes God works in the quiet through a still, small voice. And it was in God's whisper that He not only renewed Elijah's commission but also restored his hope. *El Roi* spoke firmly: "Travel back the same way you traveled here … There I want you to anoint Hazael as Aram's king, Jehu (Nimshi's son) as Israel's king, and Elisha … to replace you as prophet" (1 Kings 19:15).

Sometimes God works in the quiet through a still, small voice.

God gave Elijah very specific instructions. In those instructions, God revealed His plan. He asked Elijah to anoint men whom He would use to avenge God's name and execute divine judgment against the house of Ahab. He also revealed through those instructions that He would raise up another prophet to walk alongside and succeed Elijah, so that he would know he was not alone.

God spoke words to assure Elijah that God's purposes would prevail, and He would triumph in the end. All Elijah had to do was to listen and obey!

Are you, or is someone you love, experiencing a time of deep sadness or depression? Write below the thoughts that come to mind as you have walked through Elijah's story.

God brought you to this study not only to encourage you but also to equip you. Sometimes we know exactly why we find ourselves paralyzed by fear, hopelessness, or despair. But sometimes we experience those feelings even in the midst of great abundance and blessings. We don't understand why such emotions wash over us, and in those times, it makes our situation seem all the worse. If this is happening now, or if it happens in the future to you or someone you love, return to Elijah's story. Find comfort in *El Roi*, the One who came to Elijah and rescued him. He will do the same for you.

Find comfort in El Roi, the One who came to Elijah and rescued him. He will do the same for you.

Apply It

Elijah's story teaches practical lessons for us to tuck deep in our hearts. First, God uses ordinary people to do His work on this earth. Even the greatest of his prophets, like Elijah, were normal people whom God called to do extraordinary things. They were not spiritual giants; rather, they had ups and downs like you and me. They experienced times of great fear, despair, and yes, even depression. Isn't that comforting? I know it is to me.

Second, when we find ourselves in a pit of despair, we need not fear God, be ashamed, or run. Elijah's story shows us that we should instead turn to God. He won't rebuke us or immediately discipline us. Ours is a God of compassion and comfort who loves us with an everlasting love.

Third, God lays out specific steps we should take toward restoration. These are steps we can apply in our own circumstances, or we can use them when we walk alongside another.

El Roi …

Saw: He came to Elijah in his time of need.

Provided: He replenished Elijah with rest and nourishment.

Spoke: He issued very specific instructions for his next assignment.

Gave: He gave Elijah a companion.

If you find yourself in a place of despair, prayerfully walk through these steps one by one and allow God to do His healing work in your heart and in your circumstances.

1. Take your eyes off yourself (blame/self-pity) and instead look to *El Roi*.

2. Take care of yourself physically: Eat well, drink plenty of water, and get plenty of sleep and exercise.

3. Open your Bible and listen for God's still, small voice.

4. Pray: Talk to God about your circumstances.

5. Share your feelings with a pastor, friend, or counselor.

6. Test your perceptions: Be led by facts and truth, not your feelings.

7. Be active: Work, volunteer, and spend time with friends. Beware of isolation because it goes hand-in-hand with depression.

Part Five:
Jesus, the New Shepherd

Memory Verse: She gave this name to the LORD who spoke to her: "You are the God who sees me."

—Genesis 16:13a (NIV)

The Old Testament writers portrayed *El Roi* as a personal God, a God who cared about His people and had His eye upon them at all times. One visual image they gave us was that of a shepherd. And that image carried through to the New Testament. Old Testament prophets specifically prophesied the coming of another Shepherd, a Shepherd who would tend His flocks, gather His lambs in His arms, carry them close to His heart, and gently lead them. This coming Shepherd was Jesus.

Digging Deeper

Read each of the Old Testament verses below and share what you learn about this new Shepherd.

1. Isaiah 40:11

2. Ezekiel 34:11–16, 31 (read the entire chapter if you have time)

New Testament writers speak of Jesus as the Good Shepherd, the Chief Shepherd, the Great Shepherd of the Sheep, and the Shepherd of Our Souls. The Greek word used here is *poimen*[4] and refers not merely to one who feeds sheep; it encompasses one who tends to all the needs of the flock and oversees them day and night.

Read John 10:11–15.

Let's revisit the sheep imagery for a moment as it relates to Middle Eastern history. Sheep are helpless and unable to defend themselves against predators. They are prone to wander from the flock and need to be watched constantly. This became the role of the shepherd. The Middle Eastern shepherd *led* his sheep. He did not follow behind or walk alongside. He went before them to protect, feed, and lead them.

He knew each sheep by name. I find it interesting that it was not uncommon for a shepherd to actually name his sheep. Quite often he named them according to their characteristics. And his sheep recognized his voice when he called their name.

This is important because Jewish shepherds kept their sheep in two kinds of sheepfolds. In the country, they corralled them within a low-walled structure that had one narrow entrance in the front. They guarded that entrance throughout the night, literally laying their body across the doorway. But in town, the shepherds often used a communal corral with a professional gatekeeper who kept watch over the sheep of many shepherds. When morning came, each shepherd came to gather his sheep. He opened the door and called them out. And though intermingled with other flocks, when they heard the voice of *their* shepherd, they came because they knew their shepherd's voice.

Friend, Jesus our Shepherd works the same way. At the will of His Father, Jesus willingly laid down His life for us. As our Shepherd, He leads us and protects us. He knows us intimately and calls us by name. And just as the sheep knew their shepherd's voice, when we are in relationship with Jesus, we know our Shepherd's voice.

And just as the sheep knew their shepherd's voice, when we are in relationship with Jesus, we know our Shepherd's voice.

🖋 What adjective does Jesus put before Shepherd in John 10:11? Why do you suppose He uses this word? (You may need to reread John 10 again.)

🖋 **Now read John 10:14–15.** What does Jesus say about His knowledge of us?

Cling to Jesus' words here. Jesus says that just as He knows His Father and His Father knows Him, so He knows His sheep and His sheep know Him. The Father and Son are one, thus the knowledge Jesus speaks of here is a deep, intimate, mutual knowledge. Really, there is no more intimate knowledge than this.

That same intimate knowledge that exists between Jesus and His Father exists between Jesus and us. His knowledge penetrates to the deepest parts of our hearts, minds, and souls. Psalm 139 reveals that our relationship with Him began before we were even born.

🖋 <u>Read Psalm 139:15–16.</u> What treasures do you glean from this passage about *El Roi*, our Good Shepherd?

God knows our sin—the ugliest parts of our past, our failures, our fears and insecurities, our shortcomings, even the unmet longings of our hearts. And yet, in spite of it all, He remains our faithful Good Shepherd. *El Roi* finds us in those desperate, hurting places and shepherds us through them.

> God knows our sin—the ugliest parts of our past, our failures, our fears and insecurities, our shortcomings, even the unmet longings of our hearts. And yet, in spite of it all, He remains our faithful Good Shepherd.

El Roi shepherded one of my dearest friends through a dark night of the soul.[5] Lisa knew deep in her heart God had called her to minister to women. She had served in women's ministry at our church for years. She coordinated all of our women's events and did a stellar job. Everything she did was covered in prayer and done with a tender and loving heart. She met weekly with women to encourage and equip them on how to identify and effectively work in their calling. Working in this capacity energized and filled her like nothing else.

Over time, God closed doors for my friend to serve in our church—doors that had always been wide open. It was a "transition" time for our church—a good thing for the body overall, but not so good for Lisa. She felt as if part of a dream and calling had died. This change left her confused. Rejected. Invisible. Lacking confidence. *Where was God? What was He doing?*

This woman, who had devoted her life to teaching women how to hear God's voice, now heard nothing at all. She couldn't feel God. She couldn't see God. She couldn't understand God. The only thing she could bring herself to do was to crawl into her quiet-time chair, a rocking chair in which she has always sat and met with God each morning. God had shown up there at one time, and she desperately hoped that He would show up again. However, the chair that had once brought her joy and strength now brought nothing but silence.

Yet Lisa continued to faithfully show up. And she wanted credit for that. She showed up even though God was silent and seemingly not at work in every one of her prayer requests. As God demonstrated His faithfulness by giving her another day, she demonstrated hers by showing up for her quiet time in this chair. It made no sense to her. Morning after morning, showing up doing nothing, saying nothing, hearing nothing. But she did it. Why? Because it was all she had to cling to during that dark night of the soul.

Eventually, in personal and intimate ways, God showed up too. And through this difficult season, He taught my friend a critical, life-changing lesson. She learned that when we need God, we must return to the last place we experienced Him.

Lisa also learned a second lesson. She learned how to steward her hurt and her heartache well. She wanted to be a woman of integrity, so rather than spew forth anger and hate about the church and those who trampled on her dreams, she entrusted her broken heart to her family and a few trusted friends. We took turns sitting on her couch, praying her through. One of those women spoke very powerful words that Lisa will never forget: "I have enough faith for the both of us." What a dear friend! When we don't have faith enough to believe God, our friends are there to help us with our unbelief! Do you have a friend like that?

In obedience, Lisa held on to what she knew about God. She knew him as *El Roi*. She knew deep inside that God could see her and had not forgotten her. She knew He had a plan. He whispered (that same still small voice Elijah heard) one particular verse over her heart time and time again: "Enlarge the place of your tent, stretch your tent curtains wide, do not hold back; lengthen your cords, strengthen your stakes" (Isaiah 54:2 NIV).

At first, the verse confused Lisa. But slowly and surely, God unfolded its meaning. He wove a new tapestry into the fabric of her life. There were no new tangible open doors for women's ministry as she knew it, but conversations happened and meetings occurred that stirred hope in her heart.

God then spoke to my friend in May 2010 through the purchase of a car, of all things. She and her husband had secretly bought their son a car before his sixteenth birthday and put it in storage until the time came to reveal the surprise. One day she saw a car identical to his driving past her. Excitement filled her heart to know they had that same car tucked away for Connor, and he didn't even know it! In that moment, God used her son's car to remind Lisa that He had something special tucked away for her too. He could see exactly what it looked like, but she could not. And He would reveal it in His time.

And He did just that! He took a city girl who said she would never go to Africa and sent her where? To Africa. He stretched her right out of her comfort zone. For that season, instead of serving women, she served in global outreach in Burundi, Africa. Though this wasn't Lisa's "sweet spot" in ministry, she grew by leaps and bounds in her leadership ability. God then began to open doors for her to meet one-on-one with women. These meetings brought her such tremendous joy that she registered for and completed coaching classes to become a Christian coach and ministry consultant. She learned and absorbed everything she could to strengthen herself professionally for this new calling.

Her dead heart began beating again. Her "empty" was made "full" as God blessed her coaching ministry beyond what she could have ever thought. And in the past two years, God has brought her back full circle to women's ministry, with the added gift of leadership. She has taken on an executive level position with an international women's ministry! Did she experience a dark night of the soul? Yes. But her Shepherd faithfully led her, and what God has done on the other side is exceedingly, abundantly above all that she could have ever asked or imagined.

Perhaps you've walked through a similar season in your own life. Take a few minutes to reflect on your own story and then write down a few things you've learned about God that will help you when you experience another dark time in your soul.

Apply It

Jesus loves us deeply. He is *El Roi*. He sees us. He knows us intimately. He is aware of our every need and guides us gently in the way we should go. He offers safety and shelter from this harsh world. He is our friend and our defender.

Do you believe that if God loved us enough to lay down His life for us, He loves us enough to stay by our side in the darkest of times? We all experience periods when we walk through a "dark night of the soul" as did Elijah and Hagar and Lisa. God feels so distant that we cannot see, feel, or hear Him. But He is there. He is *always* there.

> *Do you believe that if God loved us enough to lay down His life for us, He loves us enough to not abandon us in the darkest of times?*

Hearing the voice of our Shepherd is imperative to gaining victory in tough times, though hearing His voice can often be difficult. Why? Because some of us don't know His voice. Others of us know it, but in the clamor of our busy lives, we don't recognize it. Others of us feel so far away from God that we cannot hear, or don't want to hear because we feel abandoned. These times are especially frustrating when, like Elijah, we feel we have been walking in His will and living in ways that please Him.

How do we come to know God's voice today since He is not physically walking among us?

Do you know the voice of the Good Shepherd? If you do, are you following His leading, listening to His direction? If not, why not?

Take time to review your lesson and prayerfully answer the following questions based on what you have learned from God's Word and what God has spoken into your heart throughout your time with Him.

🖋 Who is *El Roi*?

🖋 What does this mean for my life?

Prayer:

El Roi, I praise You because You are the Alpha and Omega; You alone know the beginning from the end. I sometimes can't understand my past, don't always accept my present, and often fear my future. Enable me to fix my eyes on You—to trust You with my past, to allow You to direct my steps each and every day, and to trust in You for all that my future holds.

Optional Video Study

🖋 Use the space below to note anything that stands out to you from the video teaching. You may also choose to take notes on a separate sheet of paper.

 Use the following questions as a guide for group discussion:

What one thing stood out to you most in this chapter?

How can you apply the name of God you studied this week to your own life and current situation?

Take a few moments to review this week's memory verse together. What does this verse mean to you personally?

Could you relate to any of the people or situations from the Bible that you studied this week? If so, how?

CHAPTER THREE

Jehovah Nissi: The One Who Stands Guard Over You

Prayer:

Heavenly Father, thank You that Your banner over me is love and that nothing in all creation will ever be able to separate me from Your love. Thank You that You love me with an everlasting love—I don't have to do anything to earn or keep it. It makes my heart sing to know that You are always with me and that You rejoice over me with gladness; quiet me with Your love, and rejoice over me with singing. As I study Your Word and seek to know You more, let every morning bring me word of Your unfailing love. When the battle seems too hard and the mountain too high, remind me that though the mountains be shaken and the hills be removed, Your unfailing love for me will not be shaken nor Your covenant of peace removed. Thank You that Your way is perfect, and that You are a shield to all who trust in You. Teach me more about who You are, Jehovah Nissi, as I open my heart to study another aspect of Your character. My amazing, sovereign God, You are the same yesterday, today, and forever. In Jesus' name I pray. Amen.

Part One:
A History Lesson

> **Memory Verse:** Moses built an altar and called it The
> LORD is my Banner.
>
> —Exodus 17:15 (NIV)

Jehovah Nissi, The Lord is my Banner—I had heard it before I began
to write this study, but I knew nothing about it. Interestingly,
my research led me to one of God's most beloved heroes of our
faith—Moses.

But before we delve into the actual story from which the name
Jehovah Nissi came, we must journey back to the past and spend
time with a few families we have already met. Because knowing
the history of God's people and understanding the covenant line is
significant to this name.

⟫⟫ Digging Deeper

Let's first revisit our friends Abraham and Sarah. Remember how
they longed for children, but at their age believed there was no
hope? Yet, in spite of their advanced age, God promised them a son.

🖋 **Read Genesis 15:1–6.** What did God promise?

We know from what we read earlier that Abraham and Sarah
grew impatient, so much so that Sarah manipulated circumstances
to get her way. Through that manipulation, Ishmael was born. In
this chapter, we focus not on Ishmael but on Sarah's natural-born
son Isaac, the child of the promise.

🖋 **Read Genesis 21:1–6.** What happened?

🖋 What did they name the promised child?

The young boy grew into a man and married a woman named Rebekah. Sadly, Rebekah was unable to have children. This broke Isaac's heart, so he pleaded with God on her behalf. The Lord answered Isaac's prayer, and she became pregnant.

🖋 **Read Genesis 25:19–28.** What do you learn about Isaac and Rebekah's children in this passage?

According to Jewish tradition, the oldest son inherited the property of the father. Thus, Esau, being the older of Isaac's two children, would inherit his father's property. Jacob, the younger brother, grew jealous of Esau and all that would soon belong to him.

🖋 **Read Genesis 25:29–34** and share what you learn about the birthright.

As the years passed, Isaac grew old and weak. The time came for his oldest son Esau to receive his father's inheritance and blessing. But Isaac had no idea that Esau had recklessly sold Jacob his birthright.

🖋 **Read Genesis 27.** What happened among Isaac, Jacob, and Esau?

🖋 What were the consequences of Jacob's deceitful actions?

Jacob's deceit caused Esau to despise his brother and hold a wicked grudge for what he had done. Can you blame him? Hate permeated Esau's heart to the point that he threatened to kill his brother for stealing his birthright and blessing.

When Rebekah learned of Esau's threat, she determined to protect Jacob by sending him to live with her brother, Laban. But she lied to Isaac, telling her husband that her goal was to stop Jacob from marrying a Canaanite woman. Before Jacob's departure, Isaac again prayed a blessing over his son: "May God Almighty bless you and make you fruitful and increase your numbers until you become a community of peoples. May he give you and your descendants the blessing given to Abraham so that you may take possession of the land where you now reside as a foreigner, the land God gave to Abraham" (Genesis 28:3–4 NIV). And off Jacob went.

Now Jacob led quite an exciting life, especially when it came to women. Uncle Laban had two daughters, Leah and Rachel. Jacob fell in love with Laban's youngest daughter, Rachel, but due to Laban's trickery and deception, he ended up marrying both of Laban's daughters (Genesis 29:14–30).

The story of Jacob and his wives reads like something straight off of a movie script. Rachel struggled to get pregnant, so she grew jealous of Leah, who had given Jacob four sons (Reuben, Simeon, Levi, and Judah). Rachel was not the only one plagued by jealousy.

Leah resented Rachel because she was young and beautiful and Jacob adored her. Rachel and Leah unremittingly competed with one another—each focusing on the things the other had that she herself lacked.

Oh, how I find myself doing the same thing. Not, of course, with another wife. Monty has only one wife. Poor man is stuck with me for life! Rather, I look at someone else's home, her success, her wardrobe, her career, her ministry, and I ask why I can't have that or be more like her.

Do you find yourself playing the comparison game? Share a time when you struggled with wanting what another woman had. How did you deal with it?

When we allow jealousy to infiltrate our hearts, it can damage us and our relationships. Rather than being thankful for what we have and all God has given us, we grow resentful and even bitter. We feel unworthy and insecure. And these emotions can lead to unwise decisions and sometimes even self-centered and destructive behavior. Oh, how we see this truth lived out in Jacob's family.

As Rachel witnessed Leah having son after son, she grew desperate. She finally took matters into her own hands. Sound familiar? Jacob's grandmother (Sarah) and his mother (Rebekah) had done the exact same thing. Both manipulated circumstances to get what they wanted. Now another generation of women was following in their deceptive footsteps.

Read Genesis 30:1–7. What did Rachel do, and what happened as a result?

What was her motivation? See verse 8.

When Leah could no longer have children and saw Rachel providing Jacob with children (Dan and Naphtali) through her servant girl, what did she do? She gave her personal servant to Jacob as his wife. This servant gave birth to two sons (Gad and Asher).

At this point, Jacob had fathered eight children by three different women. But it did not end there. Leah bore Jacob two more sons (Issachar and Zebulun). She also gave birth to a daughter (Dinah).

Much to Rachel's delight, God finally opened her womb, and she gave Jacob two sons of her own (Joseph and Benjamin). Jacob had twelve sons in all!

So what was going on in Jacob's heart through all of this? We receive an inner glimpse when God intervened in his life and renamed him. In ancient Israel, a person's name was linked to his or her character. Jacob's birth name meant "to follow, to be behind, supplanter" and referred to the circumstances under which he was born. Remember, Jacob and Esau were twins. Scripture reveals that in birth, Jacob held on to the heel of his older twin brother. Jacob always hated being second to Esau. He wanted what his brother had.

So Jacob stole his brother's birthright and ran. But as time passed, Jacob longed to reconcile with Esau. He needed to make things right in his heart and committed to do just that. In Genesis 32, Jacob embarked on a journey to find his long-lost brother. And along the way, God met him in a very real and tangible way.

What Jacob sensed, but did not fully understand, was that God had great plans for his life; plans set in place before time began. However, before God could fulfill those plans, He needed to radically change Jacob from the inside out. So God brought Jacob to a place of humble repentance.

Read Jacob's words in Genesis 32:10–12: "I am unworthy of all the kindness and faithfulness you have shown your servant. I had only my staff when I crossed this Jordan, but now I have become two groups. Save me, I pray, from the hand of my brother Esau, for I am afraid he will come and attack me and also the mothers with their children. But you have said, 'I will surely make you prosper and will make your descendants like the sand of the sea, which cannot be counted'" (NIV).

Jacob felt convicted of his sin and expressed remorse. But that was not enough, so God hunted him down and literally wrestled with him.

Read Genesis 32:22–31. What happened between God and Jacob?

What did Jacob ask God for in Genesis 32:26?

What was God's response in verse 28?

After Jacob's encounter with God, he lifted his eyes and saw, running toward him, his brother, Esau. Jacob was terrified and bowed to the ground seven times as Esau approached. Yet Esau embraced him instead. They both fell to the ground, weeping. Time had healed their bitter wounds and allowed a beautiful reconciliation of the brothers and their extended families.

Apply It

I pray this story will encourage you during trying times. God, in the form of a "man," wrestled with Jacob all through the night. God needed to teach Jacob a lesson in humility. Jacob fought hard, and when the man with whom Jacob was wrestling saw he could not overpower Jacob, he touched Jacob's hip in a way that crippled him. It was not that God was weaker than Jacob—God *chose* to come in the form of a man with whom Jacob could wrestle because He knew that would be the best way to humble him. Jacob had been wrestling his entire life—first with Esau, then Laban, and now God.

God rewarded Jacob's persistence. When Jacob finally acknowledged that the blessing he had stolen must ultimately come from God, he was able to fully receive it. This was Jacob's final wrestling match.

Reread Genesis 32:27–30.

True change often comes only after a time of struggle and wrestling with God. Jacob changed physically, because he would forever walk with a limp. He changed spiritually, because God humbled him. But God went one step further and changed Jacob's name to reflect his new heart. He would no longer be called Jacob. His new name would be Israel.

True change often comes only after a time of struggle and wrestling with God.

To commemorate God's work in his life up to this point, his new name, and to acknowledge the God of his fathers as his God also, Jacob built an altar and called it *El Elohe Israel*, which means "the mighty God of Israel" (Genesis 33:20). Jacob no longer called God the "God of his fathers"; he called him "the God of Israel," *his* God. God became personal for Jacob for the first time.

Are you struggling with God about something in your life? How does Jacob's story encourage you? What next steps will you take to make your heart right with God?

Do you see God as a personal God? Not the God of your church or your parents but *your* God … who loves you and has great plans for you? What does this mean for your life?

Part Two:
The Twelve Tribes of Israel

Memory Verse: Moses built an altar and called it The LORD is my Banner.

—Exodus 17:15 (NIV)

Are you ready for the next phase of the story as we continue our history lesson? Before we begin, let's review what we have learned.

God spoke to Abraham and made a covenant promise with him. After Abraham died, God spoke to Isaac (not Ishmael) and committed to fulfill that covenant promise. God impressed upon Isaac that it was Abraham's obedience that kept him in God's favor and in the place of blessing, and exhorted Isaac to walk with that same heart of obedience. If he did, God assured him that through his line, the original covenant promise would be fulfilled.

In God's timing, Isaac blessed his son, Jacob (not Esau), as the inheritor of the covenant. God later appeared to Jacob personally, identifying Himself as "the LORD, the God of your father Abraham and the God of Isaac." In this appearance, God told Jacob that the promises made to Abraham and Isaac were now his; he was the rightful heir.

These repeated affirmations of the covenant promise to Isaac and Jacob affirm that God acted with purposeful intent each and every time. God was working out His promises by restating and renewing them with the patriarch of every generation.

Now that we have the characters in place, let's examine how they obtained all that God promised. He didn't just hand everything to them on a silver platter. God required a long walk of obedience to receive what He had promised.

God commanded Jacob's (Israel's) twelve sons to divide into tribes. When they settled in the Promised Land, God allotted to each tribe—except Levi and Joseph—a parcel of land. The Levites did not own land because God set them apart to serve as His priests. And God doubled Joseph's allotment and awarded it, divided equally, to his sons, Manasseh and Ephraim. These became the twelve tribes of Israel.

Read Genesis 49. List Israel's (Jacob's) twelve sons.

Digging Deeper

God rooted Israel's identity and structure in these tribes. They camped in tribes; they traveled in tribes; they worked in tribes. And they eventually settled the land in tribes.

Read Numbers 2:1–3:16.

In Numbers 2:2, God spoke to Moses and issued specific instructions on how to design the Israelite camp: "When the Israelites set up camp, each tribe will be assigned its own area. The tribal divisions will camp beneath their family *banners* on all four sides of the Tabernacle, but at some distance from it" (NLT, emphasis added).

Did you notice the word *banner* in Moses' statement to Israel? We find banners everywhere we look. Most often we see them at sporting events. In high school gyms, cheerleaders run through them chanting a familiar school song. At colleges, organizations display them at campus venues to call attention to their group or cause. And at professional athletic events, companies plaster them around the stadium to persuade fans to buy their products. But this is not the kind of banner we are talking about here.

In the Old Testament, when we read about a banner, it refers to a tribal banner. The banner identified an individual with a family or tribe. This is consistent with God's character; He is a God of order, not confusion. And from afar, I imagine these banners captured the attention of friends and enemies alike and gave the impression of a united, formidable army.

What were these banners like? We don't know for certain. We do know that each tribe had its own banner. Some conjecture that the banners matched the color of the precious stone in which the name of that tribe was written on the ephod, the ornamental piece decorating the high priest's robe. Others believe there was a coat of arms painted on each standard, which referenced Jacob's blessing for that tribe. Others assert that each tribe's name was written on its banner.[1]

God further divided the twelve tribes into four groups, with three tribes in each group. The four groups defended the four sides of the tabernacle to protect it from invaders. God gave special instructions for the Levites. Moses divided them into clans, and they pitched their tents immediately around the tabernacle. As you picture this, remember the Israelites were always on the move, so the tabernacle and the tents were like a movable city. They had to continually set up and tear down the tabernacle and their tents, always repeating the same order each time.

Read Numbers 9:15–23. How did the Israelites know when and where to go?

God accompanied the people as a cloud, ensuring they had a constant, visible symbol of His presence. It spontaneously appeared and lifted, and at night it had the appearance of fire. Moses interpreted the meaning of the cloud's movement, and the people obeyed his leading. Through this cloud, God taught His people to always look to Him for guidance and to move on or wait at His command.

Apply It

God provides that same guidance today through the great and precious promises we find in His Word. But we must *choose* to open God's Word. We see a great example of choosing to believe God at His word in the life of Jehoshaphat, king of Judah. Three countries banded together, combining their armies, with the intent to attack Jerusalem.

> Alarmed, Jehoshaphat resolved to inquire of the LORD, and he proclaimed a fast for all Judah. The people of Judah came together to seek help from the LORD; indeed, they came from every town in Judah to seek him. (2 Chronicles 20:3–4 NIV)

Despite being alarmed, the king *resolved* to inquire of the Lord. Jehoshaphat didn't panic; he knew exactly what to do and to whom he should go in the midst of imminent danger. And not only did he go to the Lord, he called his people to fast and do the same. What a leader! What an example!

God provides guidance today through the great and precious promises we find in His Word. But we must choose to open God's Word.

99

🖋 Reflect on your own life. To what or to whom do you look for guidance in general?

🖋 What is your immediate response when you feel "alarmed"? To what or to whom do you look for direction or help?

🖋 When your "people" (husband, children, family, close friends) are alarmed, how do you respond? To what or to whom do you direct them for answers?

🖋 If you look to God's Word for guidance, how do you go about seeking direction? Give an example of a time when God directed you through His Word.

🖋 When asking God for guidance, do you struggle with the confidence to obey? How do you courageously take that first step of obedience? What has been God's response when you do?

Part Three: The First Battle

Memory Verse: Moses built an altar and called it The LORD is my Banner.

—Exodus 17:15 (NIV)

Now that we have a better understanding of the history of God's people, we reach the point in the story where we engage with *Jehovah Nissi*.

Read Exodus 16.

Moses led God's people from the Red Sea into the Desert of Sin, located on the east side of Egypt in the northwestern part of the Sinai Peninsula. As slaves in Egypt, they had not lacked for food and water or a place to rest their head. So when their wanderings in the desert with Moses stripped them of those basic provisions, they whined and complained.

May I be the first to confess, I'm an expert at grumbling and complaining. I work with a large ministry, and not too long ago, one of our staff members asked me to assist on a project. Being a type A personality, I immediately got to work. It required reading through fifty devotions and selecting several for a proposed project. Reading through these devotions written by my Proverbs 31 Ministries sisters was such a blessing. My task was to prayerfully select the few I felt would touch the hearts of our intended audience. It was tedious work; every devotion was worthy of being included! It took several readings to select my final four. After investing many hours in this labor of love, I drafted an email to my coworker with my selections.

Instead of sending the email immediately, I placed it in my draft file because the perfectionist in me wanted to read it one more time before sending it. And what do you think I found in my inbox just before I pressed *send* the next morning? An email informing me that the ministry had decided not to proceed with the project. As I read the words, feelings of frustration infiltrated my heart. As time passed, irritation replaced frustration. I had invested so much time … all for nothing. When I thought of all those hours spent reading and rereading, my irritation quickly shifted to anger. And then my anger morphed into total resentment, directed not only at my coworker but also at the people who had initiated this project and then suddenly, without warning, had trashed it. Did they not care? Oh, how I grumbled and complained!

When I finally reined in my anger, I contacted my coworker and asked if she still wanted my finished product. Her answer, "No, not at this time," was the icing on the cake! *What? Do you know how much time I put in? Do you even value my time?* (Those were my thoughts … not my words. Have you been there too?) But rather than speaking or writing these words, I said nothing. I waited to respond and saved my work in a file. The next time we communicated, I told her I had saved my work in the event we decided to proceed with the project in the future, and she responded positively.

Time has passed. My anger has dissipated. But when I look back, I'm ashamed at my reaction. The time and effort I invested in my assignment blessed me greatly. It allowed me to spend hours in God's Word, reading devotions written by some of my favorite women. God promises that when His Word goes out, it will not return void. What I created is something that I can use again, even if it's not for our ministry. Yet I had thought harshly of people I love and respect and had acted in a way contrary to what God expects of me.

What is your reaction when things don't go your way? Do you grumble and complain?

Read Philippians 2:14–16 and 1 Corinthians 10:10. How do these verses speak to the issue of grumbling? According to Paul's words in Philippians, why should we refrain from grumbling and complaining?

I pray that the next time I'm faced with a situation in which things don't go my way, I will make a better choice—the choice that will make me shine like a star in the sky, beaming God's love and mercy and grace (see Philippians 2:15).

Digging Deeper

Let's return to the Israelites in the wilderness. As their food and water supply ran low, they complained to Moses, questioning his motives for leading them out of Egypt. Their pressing need for food caused them to forget the horrible circumstances from which God had delivered them. God immediately responded to Moses' cry on behalf of His people and sent bread from heaven (*manna*).

After God provided food, the Israelites set out once more. God led them to a place called Rephidim (the supposed site of Mount Sinai). Upon their arrival, they found no water (Exodus 17:1–7). Again these ungrateful people complained to Moses. But this time they went further than just grumbling; they were ready to stone their leader. The Lord, patient and loving despite the whining and complaining, directed Moses to take the staff with which he had struck the Nile River and strike a particular rock. When Moses struck the rock, water poured out. God had once again faithfully provided.

You would think these people would get it—wouldn't you?—that they would readily trust God when circumstances appeared dire and hopeless. He had continually shown up in miraculous ways many times through the plagues, the parting of the Red Sea, the manna, and the water, to name just a few.

Even in battle, God was faithful. In the second half of Exodus 17, we witness how God intervened in their first battle. And here at this place of miraculous intervention we first see God called *Jehovah Nissi*, "The LORD is Our Banner."

Read Exodus 17:8–16.

Now that our earlier history lesson has been placed in perspective, we find the Israelites under attack from the Amalekites. Who were the Amalekites? They were the first nation Israel encountered and battled on their way to the Promised Land. They were the descendants of Jacob's brother (Genesis 36:12, 16).

Memory quiz! Who was Jacob's brother? Why would his descendants have hated the Israelites?

Amalek was Esau's grandson. So the Israelites and Amalekites were cousins of some sort, and it's obvious from this story that the animosity that began with Jacob and Esau infected future generations.

Deuteronomy 25:17–19 identifies the Amalekites as nomads (a traveling people) in the desert south of Canaan. They found the Israelites "on the road when [the Israelites] were all worn out, and they attacked those who had fallen behind and were isolated and defenseless. They showed no fear of God." It was a "sneak attack" designed to surprise the weary and unsuspecting. Their plan was to oust the Israelites and claim the territory upon which they had settled as their own.

Up to that point, God had provided for and fought for the Israelites at every turn. But God changed His tactic this time. He wanted His people to join in the battle. Moses called up Joshua to serve as commander-in-chief for God's army and told him to appoint men of his choosing to fight. (This is the first time we meet Joshua.) Then God assigned Joshua and Moses very specific roles: Joshua would fight; Moses would pray.

Before he left, Moses told Joshua, "I will stand at the crest of that hill *overlooking the battlefield* with God's staff in my hand" (Exodus 17:9). While Joshua chose his army, Moses, his brother, Aaron, and another man named Hur, climbed to the top of a hill where they could oversee the battle.

I imagine that when Moses arrived at the top of the hill, he stationed himself so that he could be seen by the people and the armies below. He held up the "rod of God," the miracle-working rod that had summoned the plagues of Egypt, parted the Red Sea, and brought forth water from a rock. This rod served as a banner, a symbol, to remind the soldiers—and all God's people—of the glorious and miraculous feats God had accomplished on their behalf.

It's no different for us, sweet friend. When we are in the midst of a battle, we must remember the great things God has done for us so that we can persevere through the unknown.

> *When we are in the midst of a battle,*
> *we must remember the great things*
> *God has done for us so that we can*
> *persevere through the unknown.*

🖋 What are some great things God has done for you—times when you have experienced His faithfulness and His provision? Make a list of those things.

🖋 Now write a prayer of gratitude for God's faithfulness.

🖋 How might remembering all that God has done for you in the past encourage you in a tough time you or someone you love may be going through?

Throughout the battle, when Moses held up the rod in his hand, Israel prevailed. However, when his arm fell, the Amalekites prevailed. Aaron and Hur noticed how Moses' arm grew weary, so they took a large stone and placed it under him. (Don't you find it interesting that Moses sat on a rock, another name and another visible symbol for our God?) More importantly, Aaron and Hur continually held up Moses' hands—one on one side and one on the other—so that his hands and the rod remained high and lifted up until sunset. Because of the faithfulness of these four men, the Israelites won their first battle as God's people!

The outcome of the battle did not rest on one man or the other: Joshua or Moses; the man of the sword or the man of prayer. God worked through the two, in tandem, to give His people victory.

What followed the battle? First, Moses honored *God* ... not the soldiers, not Joshua, but God. He built an altar to God and called it "The LORD is my Banner" (Exodus 17:15 NIV), referring to the lifting of the rod in his hand as their banner. He wanted the Israelites to forever remember, confess, and acknowledge God as The Banner, the One who watches over and guards His people, the One who is the strength of His people.

Psalm 20:5 speaks to this same truth: "May we shout for joy over your victory and lift up our banners in the name of our God" (NIV). David wrote this psalm, recording the words of the people just before he went into battle.

Second, God ordered Moses to write down the account of this victory so that it would never be forgotten. God specifically asked that Joshua read what Moses had written.

Throughout the Israelites' wandering in the desert, the Amalekites remained staunch enemies of God's people. It was not until David's reign that they would finally be destroyed (1 Samuel 30). God promised this in His message to Moses when He said He would "completely blot out the name of Amalek from under heaven" (Exodus 17:14b NIV).

Let us never forget that we have a God who fights for His people. He will exact justice from anyone who touches or harms the apple of His eye. Isaiah 54:17 says, "'No weapon forged against you will prevail, and you will refute every tongue that accuses you. This is the heritage of the servants of the LORD, and this is their vindication from me,' declares the LORD" (NIV). God once again proved Himself faithful in watching over and providing for His people.

Let us never forget that we have a God who fights for His people. He will exact justice from anyone who touches or harms the apple of His eye.

Read Zechariah 2:8–10. Write down these verses in your own words.

Read Deuteronomy 25:19. What does Moses say to the people of God?

For a bit more perspective here, let's review Moses' early years. His mother, a Levite woman, gave birth to him during the same time that Pharaoh ordered all male Israelite babies be killed. She kept him for three months and then, fearing for his life, she placed him in a basket and hid him among the reeds in the Nile River. Pharaoh's daughter found the boy and adopted him as her own. She named him Moses. When he grew up and learned the truth about who he was, he killed an Egyptian whom he found beating a fellow

Israelite. Pharaoh heard about this and sent men to kill Moses. Moses, knowing his life was in danger, fled to Midian.

🪶 **Read Exodus 2:15–22; 3:1.** Who is Jethro?

🪶 Whom did Moses marry?

During the battle with the Amalekites, Moses sent his wife and children away to be with Jethro. After the battle, when Jethro heard of all that God had done for Moses and his people, he sent word to Moses that he was bringing his family back to him. Overjoyed, Moses went out to meet them. He told his father-in-law everything the Lord had done for the Israelites, recounting the hardships and miracles.

🪶 **Read Exodus 18:10–11.** Summarize Jethro's response.

Upon hearing Moses' story, Jethro gave a powerful testimony revealing his conviction of Yahweh's superiority over all other gods. His confession made clear that God's work that day went far beyond the battlefield. Indeed, God had a plan and purpose for every life, drawing people to Himself through His miraculous acts. Jethro was one of those people, and he did not just gain a stronger faith in God; he played an important role in Israelite history, giving Moses wise advice that formulated the early stages of an organized judicial system that we still utilize today!

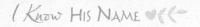

What advice did Jethro give Moses (Exodus 18:13–26)?

⟩⟩ Apply It

When Moses faced his very first battle in the wilderness, God did not fight the battle for him. Instead, God engaged His people in the battle. He invited them to join Him in His work. They were faithful to do their part, God was faithful to do His, and it led to a great victory.

Every army in the world fights under a flag. We know that the flag, in and of itself, has no power. It signifies that the soldiers fighting under it are backed by a nation whose power and resources are at their disposal.

We Christians stand under the flag or banner of *Jehovah Nissi*. And at our disposal are all the riches, treasures, resources, and power of Almighty God.

> *We Christians stand under the flag or banner of Jehovah Nissi. And at our disposal are all the riches, treasures, resources, and power of Almighty God.*

What struggles are you facing? Are you fighting temptations that seem greater than you can bear? Are you fighting for a marriage that seems hopeless? Are you suffering from a chronic sickness that strips you of all strength and you feel as if you cannot endure even one more day? Are you being pressured to make decisions that will not honor God? Tell God your struggles. If it will help you, write them out below.

I don't know what battle you are facing or who your Amalek is, but God does. I want to encourage you, though, to stand under God's banner; fly it with confidence over your heart and your home. Trust Him to fight with you and for you. And keep this message close to your heart as we head into the next lesson.

Part Four:
Prayer Wins the Battle

Memory Verse: Moses built an altar and called it The LORD is my Banner.

—Exodus 17:15 (NIV)

Moses did not enlist in God's army as a soldier. He did not choose who would go to battle. He didn't even design the battle plan. God called Moses to do one thing. In the face of impending destruction, God called Moses to pray.

Although essential to any battle, prayer is one of the hardest ways to contribute. Physically taking up arms and participating gives us some sense of control over the outcome. But standing back and praying often feels like it's just not enough. We want to "do something." But there are times when prayer and prayer alone is all that God needs or asks of us.

During our daughter Lauren's seventh grade school year, her pediatrician diagnosed her with scoliosis (curvature of the spine). It took her father and me by surprise because we couldn't detect any noticeable curve in her back. Lauren's pediatrician referred us to a pediatric orthopedic spine specialist who took a battery of X-rays. The doctor called us out into the hall to view them. As I viewed the X-rays, my stomach lurched. I could not believe what I was seeing. Lauren's spine perfectly resembled the letter "S." Fear flooded my heart. *Surely this was not her X-ray. Surely it was a horrible mistake.*

The specialist confirmed it was indeed Lauren's spine. Her curves had progressed enough to require a back brace that she would need to wear twenty-three hours a day, seven days a week. The doctor further explained the diagnosis and instructed us where to go to be measured for the brace. It felt as if someone had punched me in the gut. Tears fell as we walked out of the office in silence. What does a mother say to a brokenhearted thirteen-year-old girl who had just received such a life-changing diagnosis?

How could this be? The days, weeks, and months following this shocking news were some of my hardest days as a mother.

Despite wearing the brace for nearly a year and receiving two years of chiropractic care, Lauren's curves continued to worsen. By age fifteen, she was suffering from extreme back pain, so we sought a second opinion. Our new doctor X-rayed her back again and pronounced that surgery was her only option.

Throughout this process, we prayed fervently for healing; as instructed in the Word of God, I anointed my sweet girl with oil and prayed healing prayers over her; we called upon elders who prayed over her, but we saw no improvement. Lauren struggled to understand God's plan. And although I trusted God with my girl, I had some fist-shaking moments, especially in her darkest times. She suffered with back pain day and night. Sometimes she needed to stand in the back of her classroom to relieve the pain. The scoliosis resulted in her having to quit competitive cheerleading and even limited the role she could play in high school cheerleading. Lauren became angry with God.

Now I wasn't just praying for her physical healing; I felt as if I was in a battle for my girl's faith. Night after night, I lay by her side, listening to her cries, begging God to do something, *anything* to intervene. I was her mother, the one who was supposed to fix things and make them better. But there seemed to be nothing I could do. I felt helpless. Fear filled my heart as I thought about doctors carving open my baby girl's back from the nape of her neck to the curve of her hips. *Where would I find the strength to support her through this surgery? How would I watch them roll her away? How would I sit through the six to eight hours as they surgically inserted rods and screws into her spine? How would I watch her endure days and weeks of excruciating pain and suffering? Why her, Lord? Why our family? I can't do this, Lord. I can't do this!*

Night after night I allowed my mind to travel to these places. Tears flowed incessantly. My sleep was restless. I awakened nearly every night asking my Lord: *Why? Why does she have to deal with so much at the tender age of sixteen?*

My rational side reasoned it could be worse—so much worse. Many mothers have children who are battling cancer and chronic illnesses; some of those children died. I have walked alongside of, cried with, and prayed for many of these mothers. And more often than not, rational thoughts prevailed. Lauren will recover; she will be strong and healthy again. This is just a blip on the screen.

But then my reality, the reality of my emotions and fears, forced its way back into my heart. I wanted to believe. I wanted to understand. I wanted to trust. But the whys and the what-ifs overrode every rational thought. Have you been there?

> *I wanted to believe. I wanted to understand. I wanted to trust. But the whys and the what-ifs overrode every rational thought. Have you been there?*

I was exhausted. I tried to be strong. After all, I'm a speaker and Bible teacher. How could I be anything but strong and trusting? But as the surgery grew closer, my heart grew heavier and heavier, my tears flowed easier and easier, until one day at work I could hold it in no more. I found a dear friend and poured out my heart to her. As dear sisters in Christ often do, she grabbed my hand and prayed.

She asked the Lord to provide for my every need, and then she specifically prayed that provision would come *through friends and family, through those to whom I had ministered.* She knew I had a devotion running on the Proverbs 31 Ministries website the next day in which I shared Lauren's story. She seemed convinced that someone would reach out to me based on that devotion.

I awoke the next morning having no idea how powerfully God would answer my friend's prayer. He answered it in accordance with Ephesians 3:20—exceedingly and abundantly more than we could have ever asked or imagined!

> Now to the God who can do so many *awe-inspiring things, immeasurable things,* things greater than we ever could ask or imagine through the power at work in us. (Ephesians 3:20)

The comments and emails from my Bible study girlfriends and my Proverbs 31 Ministries family fed my thirsty soul. Some provided rich Scriptures and promises from God. Some shared prayers. Others shared scoliosis surgery stories that gave me great hope and confirmed the decisions we had made. Others shared personal stories of hope and God's provision. God gave me manna; He miraculously provided what I needed, what I could not find on my own because I was tired and weary!

Just one day before Lauren's surgery, a precious woman in my Bible study dropped by with a gift. Inside the beautifully wrapped box, I found two handmade elegantly decorated boxes filled with feathers. What a strange gift we thought, until we read her prayer:

> *You are the Almighty Most High and You offer us shelter and refuge when we trust You. Father, I ask this promise from You for Wendy and Lauren. Please cover them with Your feathers, and under Your wings may they find a dwelling place. Like the wings of a mother bird, may the shadow of Your protection rest over them, keeping them safe and sure. When fear assails*

*and their cares trouble them, gently remind them that they have ventured
out of that protecting shadow.*

The morning of Lauren's surgery, we awakened at 4:30 a.m. My
stomach still churned. As Lauren freely expressed her fears, her dad
and I listened to each and every one and did our best to provide
the strength she needed. We arrived at the hospital to be met by
a wonderful team of people who surrounded us with the very best
of care. Lauren fought back the tears as long as she could, but they
finally erupted when the nurse inserted the IV in her hand. To calm
her, they gave her medicine that launched a bout of giggling, which
lasted until they rolled her through the doors of the OR. As they
took my precious baby girl away, I wanted to burst through those
doors, scoop her into my arms, and run all the way home. Yet I
knew the Lord had brought us to this place to trust Him. I really
had to live it—no more talking about it; no more writing about it;
no more teaching about it. I had to live it.

As we waited, God filled our cup as friends filled the room,
a few at a time, in perfect time. One would leave, another would
come. Friends to pray, friends to laugh, friends to cry. Texts and
phone messages poured in, each with its own encouraging word.

I prayed for the Lord to provide at least one believing person in
the OR that morning. Who knew that He would again give abundantly more than I could ever ask or imagine? Lauren's surgeon
allowed her Young Life leader, an orthopedic nurse, to observe
the surgery. Holly stood by Lauren the entire time, observing and
praying over my sweet girl for seven and a half hours! When the
orthopedic surgeon at last walked back into the waiting room that
afternoon, he had a big grin on his face, "The surgery was a complete success," he said.

Later that night, I lay by Lauren's side in the hospital bed as she cried out in pain, "Mommy, please pray. Please ask God to make this pain go away."

The first few days at home were difficult and, at times, almost unbearable. But each day, Lauren's pain decreased and her strength increased. God continued to provide. Although I was weary and exhausted, God took me to a place that I will never forget, a place of complete and utter dependence on Him. I felt so helpless, yet He swooped in and covered us under the shadow of His wing, just as the woman's feather-covered prayer said He would.

Jehovah Nissi, The LORD is My Banner, provided for us in so many ways, but one of the main ways was through prayer. He did not answer our prayers for healing in the way I thought He should or would, but He supplied so much more. I want to leave you with a beautiful memory. Through the prayers of my Proverbs 31 Ministries sisters (who committed to pray hour by hour throughout her surgery), through an amazing scrapbook created by my beloved Bible study girls, through a blanket I brought to the hospital embroidered with Psalm 63:7, and through a vivid dream I had one night, God gently reminded me in real and powerful ways that we were under His Banner ... under the covering of His feathers ... under the shadow of His wing.

Digging Deeper

Moses set an example for us to follow. When we face a battle, as I did with Lauren, sometimes the most effective action to take, the most powerful way to see God move, is to pray, pray, and pray some more.

Let's examine the steps Moses took upon learning of the battle against the Amalekites.

Set Yourself Apart

Moses is not the only man of God who took a stand ("on top of the hill," Exodus 17:9b NIV) and prayed. Habakkuk stood atop a high place to look and listen for answers to the complaints he had poured out to God. He set himself apart from his community to get alone with God.

Read Habakkuk 2:1. Write this verse in your own words.

It's no different for us. When we want to hear from God; when we want to see Him at work in our circumstances; when we want answers to our questions, we must set ourselves apart in a quiet place. It may not be a tower. It may be a closet, a retreat center, a back porch, or soft ground shaded by a tree. Coming apart from the world creates time and space for unhindered prayer.

Coming apart from the world creates time and space for unhindered prayer.

Our quiet moments with God open our ears to hear and our hearts to receive the truths that will pierce the silence and combat the lies. To resolve the questions that might arise when we don't understand His plans and are perplexed by His methods.

Read Psalm 5:3 and 86:1–7. What do these verses say about sitting quietly before the Lord and inclining our ears to hear?

Be Alert

Standing watch, by definition, requires readiness and alertness. Moses stood and kept watch: "I will stand" (Exodus 17:9b NIV). He waited and listened. Likewise, when we pray, we must be on alert. We have a very real enemy who prowls around like a roaring lion, waiting to pounce.

Read Ephesians 6:18 and 1 Peter 5:8. Make a brief list of what these verses say about alertness.

Standing guard, prepared in heart and mind, ensures our readiness for the enemy and his tactics. When we sense an attack, we will know to sound the alarm so that we, and those we love, can stand firm against his efforts.

Standing guard, prepared in heart and mind, ensures our readiness for the enemy and his tactics.

Pray with Authority

The staff Moses used that day on the mountain was the one God had given him when He called Moses to lead the Israelites out of Egypt. He led the battle "with the staff of God in my hands" (Exodus 17:9 NIV).

Read Exodus 4:1–5. What went on between God and Moses in this exchange?

Moses' staff served as a symbol of Moses' authority and legitimized his leadership and his call as God's chosen one to free the Israelite people. Moses used God's staff to accomplish amazing miracles (Exodus 7–14). We have that same authority today, only we don't have a staff. We have something better: the Word of God. His Word is a powerful weapon in our hands. He sent it so that we could wield it in every battle. It's our authority against all enemies.

Don't Do It Alone

Did you notice that Moses did not go to the "top of the hill" alone? Aaron and Hur went with him (Exodus 17:10).

Likewise, God does not intend for us to do this thing called life alone. When I was walking with Lauren through her scoliosis journey, I went too long trying to face the situation alone. After all, aren't we supposed to be able to stand strong through anything because we are Christians? Doesn't God's Word tell us that we can do all things through Him who strengthens us?

God does not intend for us to do this thing called life alone.

Yes, but "one another" verses also fill those very same pages. These Scriptures teach us to come alongside one another, to love one another, minister to one another, comfort one another, and pray for one another. Sometimes we forget these verses and try to fight our battles alone so that we aren't a burden or don't appear weak.

That day on the mountain, God called Moses to a huge task, to pray his army through a tough battle. In time, he grew weary as he tried to hold his arms up for hours on end.

What happened when Moses lowered his arms? (See Exodus 17:11–12.)

Can you think of another time when a man of God called upon friends to strengthen and pray for Him in His time of need? (See Matthew 26:36–46.) What happened?

What difference do you think it would have made in Jesus' last hours if His friends had stayed up and prayed?

If Jesus Himself needed prayer in His time of need, how much more do we? There are times when we need a team of people praying and interceding on our behalf.

If Jesus Himself needed prayer in His time of need, how much more do we?

I love this acronym we use in our Proverbs 31 Ministries Online Bible study family:

T—Together
E—Everyone
A—Achieves
M—More

Do you have friends to come alongside you in prayer? If you don't, pray for God to bring some prayer warriors into your life. Do you come alongside others in prayer? If you don't, pray for God to show you people in your sphere of influence for whom you can pray and with whom you can join together in prayer.

Write It Down

Finally, God instructed Moses to document Israel's victory, saying, "Write this on a scroll as something to be remembered" (Exodus 17:14a NIV). He specifically wanted Joshua to hear about the prayer. Joshua needed to know that he did not win that battle alone. It was won through prayer *and* might working in tandem. Just as Moses' example, God wants us to journal what He has done for us so we will remember and gain strength for the next trial.

My friend, in times of doubt, despair, confusion, weakness, anger, and disbelief, come apart. Be alert. Pray. Call on friends. And write down what God has done.

Apply It

As Lauren lay in bed recovering those days and weeks following her surgery, I shared with her the name of every visitor—what they brought and what they prayed. I read her the many texts and emails we received. I shared my journal entries. I wanted her to see God's hand all along the way so that she would remember for next time ... so that *I* would remember for next time. Because, my friend, next time will come.

As we wrap up this discussion about prayer, let me ask you a couple of questions.

Are you recording your prayers? What about answers to those prayers?

Are you willing to share how God has worked in your life through prayer to encourage others who find themselves in a difficult place?

If you have never done so or haven't done so recently, take some time to reflect on how God has worked in your life through prayer. Then write down what you remember, or share with a friend a time in your life when God worked through your prayers to bring you through trying circumstances.

Part Five:
The Cross

> **Memory Verse:** Moses built an altar and called it The
> LORD is my Banner.
>
> —Exodus 17:15 (NIV)

We all face times when the challenges and demands of everyday
life sap our physical, emotional, and even spiritual strength. Our
reserves become depleted. But God is faithful. He provides for us
today just as He did for Moses.

Just as the staff served as Moses' banner in his battles, the cross
of Christ serves as our banner. Through the cross, God reminds us
of one very important truth—a truth I want us to never ever forget.
In Christ, we are more than conquerors. We are overcomers!

Read Romans 8:37. Write this verse in your own words. Share
what it means in your life, whether in a past, current, or future
situation.

Exodus 17 doesn't simply document the Israelites' first battle
after crossing the Red Sea. If we believe that, we totally miss the
meaning of Exodus and, really, the entire Old Testament. God,
through His Holy Spirit, spoke through individuals such as Moses
not to give us mere history lessons but that we might understand
Him more and know the hope that we have in Him.

Read Romans 15:4. What does it say?

Digging Deeper

We engage in battles every day. As wives and mothers, sisters and grandmothers, friends and colleagues, we will experience frustration, anger, unforgiveness, suffering, sickness, despair, and even death. Often, the behavior of others will turn our lives upside down. Many of you can probably understand when I say I have had days where I simply wanted to walk out the door of my home and never come back. On more than one occasion, I have asked God: *Why? Why is this happening? What good can come from this?*

We need to gird ourselves for these battles. Whether they are big or small, we need to be prepared. How do we do that? How do we ready ourselves for the difficult times that we're all sure to face? First, we invite Jesus into our lives. It's Him living in us that gives us strength for whatever comes our way. Second, we store up His Word in our hearts. We read His Word. We rehearse His Word. We recall His Word, for that is what equips us to be more than conquerors. Let's take a look now at what specific instructions Jesus gave us for facing these battles.

Recognize the Enemy

God defines our enemy in Ephesians 6:12: "We're not waging war against enemies of flesh and blood alone. No, this fight is against tyrants, against authorities, against *supernatural* powers *and demon princes that slither* in the darkness of this world, and against wicked *spiritual armies* that lurk about in heavenly places."

According to Ephesians 6:12, who or what is our enemy?

What does 1 Peter 5:8 say about our enemy?

If you see your enemy not as flesh and blood, how can it change how you respond in a battle?

Years ago when our daughter Lauren was in middle school, we attended a worship service in which our pastor's wife spoke on this very topic. She explained how easy it is to see our husbands, our children, our families, even our churches as the enemy. It's human nature to attack when provoked, sometimes even when not provoked. But when we realize that Satan is the true enemy, we gain a new perspective. It's Satan, the father of lies, who is at work seeking to destroy our marriages, divide our families, and eradicate our friendships. It was a good message. One I agreed with wholeheartedly.

After the service, we went to our favorite burger place, as we often do. During the drive home, we decided to take a scenic route around a beautiful lake near our home. But what we intended as a peaceful drive turned into a dramatic manifestation of the message we had just heard. Our children, who are generally really good kids, began to banter in fun—at first. We could see it taking a bad turn as Lauren, our older child, got a bit bolder and more biting with her sarcasm. My husband intervened and asked the kids to stop talking, slightly elevating his tone to arrest their arguing. Rather than obey, Lauren told her father that they were fine and could "work it out on their own." But they did not work it out on their own.

Now beyond angry, my husband stepped back in: "Be quiet. I don't want to hear another word." Lauren, of course, said another word. Does this sound familiar to those of you with children? I know it does; I can just see you nodding your head in agreement!

Tires screeching, my husband pulled over to the side of the road. He ordered Lauren out of the car. With a huge huff, she reluctantly opened the door and stepped out. I knew this would not end well because they were both seething by this time. But something in me caused me to speak up. "Monty, would you mind if I spoke to her instead of you?"

He looked over at me. "Why?"

I said, "I'm not sure, but I feel like I'm supposed to address this based on what our pastor's wife said today."

He nodded yes, so I got out of the car and walked over to Lauren. She had that look teenagers get. Arms tightly folded; jaw firmly set; neck rigidly stiff; eyes narrowed, filled with disgust. Not far from us was a swing, overlooking the lake. I encouraged her, "Let's go sit." She reluctantly followed. When we got to the swing, these words poured forth:

> Lauren, do you remember how we just learned that our battle is not against flesh and blood but against the powers of this dark world. Against Satan? The truth of that message is coming alive in our midst right now. We were having a fun day, and Satan didn't like it. He decided to bring his ugly, lying, deceitful self into our car today. And we allowed it. He moved you to disobey and talk back. He moved your father to lose his temper and speak harshly. You both spoke words that you cannot take back. You are a wonderful daughter. You're kind; you have an obedient heart; and you love your family. Your dad is a good man and a loving father. He loves you so much. Don't let Satan win today, Lauren. See him

for who he is. Don't let him divide our family and win this battle today. You are God's girl, and you can overcome anything Satan throws at you by the power of the Holy Spirit that lives in you.

As I spoke, her jaw released; her arms loosened; her neck relaxed. I asked if I could pray with her. Eyes lowered, but no longer narrowed, she mumbled yes. As I prayed, I kept my eyes locked on her. As the words flowed from my mouth, tears fell from her eyes. Her heart softened. She placed her hand on mine in a powerful moment of complete surrender.

As I said "Amen," we hugged and walked back to the car. She went directly to her daddy and asked for his forgiveness and gave him a big hug. He too asked for forgiveness. They hugged again. We got back in the car and drove home.

God brought His Word alive that day in our car! And that old devil … he was nowhere in sight!

Is there someone in your life who you see as "the enemy"? Identify that person and share what it is that makes him or her your enemy.

What is one step you can take toward resolving your situation and giving God the victory, not Satan?

Be Alert

First Peter 5:8 begins with these words, "Be alert and of sober mind" (NIV). The King James Version says, "Be sober, be vigilant." *Sober* translates from the Greek word *nepho*, which means "to be free from the influence of intoxicants."[2] This brings to mind another word with which we are familiar: *sobriety*. *Sober* speaks of sobriety of mind. We must be mentally self-controlled. *Vigilant* translates from the Greek word *gregoreo* and means "to keep awake, to watch."[3] Peter encouraged the persecuted church to be alert, self-controlled, and vigilant in prayer.

Watch for and be alert for whom? The devil. The word *Satan* means "adversary," and the word *devil* means "the accuser, the slanderer."[4] We have an enemy of our souls, and we must be prepared for the lies, accusations, battles, and troubles he will send our way.

Ephesians 6:12 teaches that Satan has a host of demons who accompany him in his fight against us. This is why Peter calls us to be "sober" and "alert." We must prepare in advance for our battles so that we will be ready for any assault Satan brings against us.

Put On the Armor of God

Being prepared is usually not something I have a problem with. In college, I began studying for my exams weeks before they were scheduled. No all-nighters for me. I need my sleep! Some of you may know that I'm an attorney by trade. For the bar exam, I created a comprehensive study schedule that started months before the test. Nowadays, I love to host parties at my house. I clean, organize, shop, and decorate days ahead so that all I need to do the day of is cook and bake. Sometimes I even finish cooking and baking the day before the party. Type A personality? Absolutely! But it works for me and keeps me from being stressed before big events. It gives me room for any unexpected circumstances should they arise.

I must confess that I didn't always approach my spiritual life with the same diligence. In fact, it wasn't until the last few years that I truly understood the significance of implementing the same kind of preparation in my spiritual life. But raising teenagers will get you there quickly!

Whatever our battle, Ephesians 6 tells us to draw our strength and might from God (verse 10) and not the world. Second Corinthians 10:3–4 says, "For though we live in the world, we do not wage war as the world does. The weapons we fight with are not the weapons of the world. On the contrary, they have divine power to demolish strongholds" (NIV).

We find the weapons God speaks of in Ephesians 6. He directs us to put on the whole armor of God. We need His armor to fight those unseen enemies—the ones strategically hidden from our view. Accordingly, Paul tells us that God gives us these weapons so that we can stand firm no matter when, where, or how the enemy attacks.

Read Ephesians 6:13b. What does this verse indicate will happen if we put on every piece of God's armor in preparation for our battle?

Read Ephesians 6:14–17. List the six pieces of armor and what they represent.

God desires that we deepen our walk with Him, to grow spiritually in such a way that we will be able to lead and guide others as they seek to know Him the way we know Him. Satan opposes that growth, and unless we prepare for our battles with him, both offensively and defensively, he will prevail. We must put on each piece of armor *every day*. We must gain a firm grasp of God's Word. We must intentionally set time aside to worship and pray. When we engage in these disciplines, we will not only hold our ground, but we will emerge victorious each and every time.

When sharing about a trial in her own life, Anne Graham Lotz closed her message with this question: How have you reacted to the storm? She then told a most interesting story about a turkey and an eagle. She compared how each reacted to the threat of a storm. A turkey reacts by running under the barn, hoping the storm won't come near it. The eagle, on the other hand, leaves the security of its nest and spreads its wings to ride the air currents of the approaching storm, knowing the wind will carry it higher in the sky than it could possibly soar on its own.[5]

So when considering how you react to the storms of life, which are you? A turkey? Or an eagle? Share why.

Pray the Sword of the Spirit: God's Word

Read Ephesians 6:18. What is the last instruction God gives on how to stand firm in our spiritual battles?

Since we are studying the names of God, let's examine another of God's names. Did you know one of God's names is the Commander of the Lord's Armies? It's by this name that the Lord identified Himself to Joshua in Joshua 5:14.

Read Joshua 5:13–15.

Joshua served as the human commander of the Israelite army. But standing before Joshua was the Divine Commander—the true Commander not only of the Israelite army but of all God's armies!

Scholars maintain that this is another preincarnate appearance of the Lord Jesus Christ.[6] Did you notice that this "Man" had his sword drawn? The sword signified that the Lord Himself would be fighting for Joshua and the people of Israel.

Joshua's reaction? He fell face down and worshiped. He knew that he was in the presence of God.

God spoke these words to another great man of God. Who was it? (See Exodus 3:5.)

The Commander of the Lord's Armies still has His sword drawn today. And you hold that sword in your hand right now, my friend. It's your Bible. It is now our weapon. God uses it to fight through us. Indeed, Ephesians 6:17 tells us that the sword of the Spirit, which is the word of God, is our *only* offensive weapon. As long as we keep our Bible in our hand and His Word hidden in our heart, we will never be defenseless!

As long as we keep our Bible in our hand and His Word hidden in our heart, we will never be defenseless!

When children of God pray God's Word, we fight against evil with the full force of the Commander of the Lord's Armies behind us. We are more than conquerors through Him.

What encouragement do you find from Joshua's story?

Apply It

Our story does not end here. Revelation 19:15 promises that the Commander of the Lord's Armies will one day come again, this time with "a sharp sword" darting forth out of His mouth.

Read Revelation 19:11–16. What emotions do these words elicit as you read them?

On that day, the Rider on the white horse will, by His Word alone, crush all evil, bind Satan in chains, and cast him into the deep abyss (Revelation 20:1–3). Although at times we feel as if evil wins out, in the end it will not. Satan will fall. Jesus will triumph. That drawn sword is a guaranteed victory, not just for Joshua, but for us as well!

One day, *all* will bow down before *Jehovah Nissi*. Not a single man or woman will remain standing in His presence. You see, He is the King of kings and Lord of lords (Revelation 19:16). He has all authority on heaven and on earth.

What does it mean for you to know God is the Commander of the Lord's Armies? How does this truth speak into the challenges you face right now?

Does what you read in Revelation 19 affect how you think about death and eternity? If so, how?

Take time to review your lesson and prayerfully answer the questions below based on what you have learned from God's Word and what God has spoken into your heart throughout your time with Him.

Who is *Jehovah Nissi*?

What does this mean for my life?

⟩⟩ Prayer:

Jehovah Nissi, thank You for raising a standard over me as I face battles of many kinds: physical, spiritual, mental, and emotional. Give me the mind of Christ. Enable me to stand and fight, not in my own strength, but in the power of Your Holy Spirit. Grant me victory in the name of Your Son, Jesus.

Optional Video Study

Use the space below to note anything that stands out to you from the video teaching. You may also choose to take notes on a separate sheet of paper.

Use the following questions as a guide for group discussion:

What one thing stood out to you most in this chapter?

How can you apply the name of God you studied this week to your own life and current situation?

Take a few moments to review this week's memory verse together. What does this verse mean to you personally?

Could you relate to any of the people or situations from the Bible that you studied this week? If so, how?

CHAPTER FOUR

Jehovah Rapha: The One Who Heals You

Prayer:

Heavenly Father, God Our Healer, unveil in fresh new ways the truth of this facet of who You are. I have experienced unanswered healing prayers. Because of that, I have questions. I have doubts. Teach me. Challenge my simple faith to go deeper and ask hard questions. Reveal new truths to me and grant me the wisdom and knowledge to understand them. Thank You that You are forever with me ... that even when I feel confused, alone, and forgotten, You promise to go before me, walk alongside me, and be my rear guard. There is nowhere I can go that You are not. Help me to experience Your amazing healing power. Teach me how to cast my burden on You and allow You to sustain me as I wait on You. Help me to quiet my heart and still my mind. Enable me to rest in You. Help me to be joyful in hope, patient in affliction, and faithful in prayer. I ask all this in Jesus' powerful and effective name. Amen.

Part One:
When God Doesn't Heal

> **Memory Verse:** I am the LORD, who heals you.
>
> —Exodus 15:26b (NIV)

Imagine three little girls giggling, laughing, playing make believe, having a big time in their yard. Maria, the youngest, can't quite lift herself up on the monkey bars, but she so desperately wants to! Suddenly she hears her older brother, Will, pulling into the driveway. Maria knows he will help her. As she sees the car round the corner, heading for the garage, Maria, filled with excitement, runs toward the car, calling her brother's name, "Will! Will!" Of course, Will cannot see or hear his sister as her tiny body runs full speed toward the large SUV.

What happened next is heartbreaking.

Her older sister screamed, "Maria! Stop!"

Maria kept running.

Her sister desperately cried out her name again and began waving her arms and running toward the car. She knew there was no way her brother could see Maria.

Mom was inside. She heard screams—not the kind of screams that result from a bug crawling across your path or getting irritated with your little sister. These were the stop-you-dead-in-your-tracks screams. She tore through the house and out the back door. Once outside, she saw her son cradling his youngest sister in his arms ... both of them covered in blood.

"Mom! I hit her with the car."

She gently lifted Maria from Will's arms and cradled her as they waited for help to arrive. Blood streamed from every crevice of her body. Mom began rescue breathing. When there seemed no response, she momentarily stopped and pounded her fist into the ground, pleading for God to save her baby. Within moments, her husband arrived and took over the rescue breathing until a paramedic arrived.

The EMTs loaded Maria onto a stretcher, continuing to work on her limp and bloodied body. They then loaded her into a Life Flight helicopter. Friends took Mom and Dad to the hospital.

Upon their arrival, Maria's doctors greeted them and took them, not to the bustling emergency room triage area to which Maria had been brought, but to a cold, empty room off to the side. It was there the doctors began the speech—they were so sorry, they had done all they could, but they could not save her.

"No!" Mom screamed. "No!"

Moments later, doctors led them into the trauma room where the nurses had disconnected most of the equipment that had been used to try and save Maria's life. They saw their baby lying there, as if she was asleep, with only one small abrasion on her forehead.

Dad cried out, "Oh, God! Breathe life into Maria!" He pleaded, "You can bring her back to life! Please bring her back to life!" He knew God could do so if He chose.

Mom knew that too. But something inside her knew that God had healed Maria in another way, a way they didn't want. She walked up to her husband and whispered, "We've got to let her go, Sweetie. It's okay to let her go. It's time to let her go."

This tragic and heartbreaking story is real. The father and mother are Steven Curtis Chapman, the Grammy Award–winning singer/songwriter, and his wife, Mary Beth. In her book, *Choosing to See,* Mary Beth writes, "Somehow in that unthinkable moment it became clear to Steven and me that we were standing at the very door of heaven, placing our little girl carefully in the arms of Jesus,

desperately trusting that she would be safe there until we could come and join her."[1]

Steven shares the words he spoke to the doctors and nurses surrounding them in the trauma room that day: "As crazy as this seems right now, the only thing I can say to honor the life of my little girl and our terrible loss at this moment is to ask you, please don't miss this ... we will all stand here one day and face eternity. If you don't know the One who can give you eternal life, His name is Jesus ... you need to meet Him and you really need to meet my little girl in heaven ... she's amazing."[2]

The couple then bent over and kissed their baby girl's forehead. Mary Beth, hand shaking, stroked Maria's sweet face and tucked her hair back behind her ear one last time. Then they walked out to begin their long journey of grieving, waiting for the day they would be with their daughter once again.

Why didn't God just reach down and stop Will's truck that day? Why didn't He make Mary Beth's rescue breathing work? Why didn't God use the doctors to save their baby girl? Why didn't God answer her daddy's cry to bring her back to life? After all, He is able. He is God the Healer. He is the same yesterday, today, and forever.

They were committed believers who worked in full-time ministry. Through his music, Steven Curtis Chapman had ministered to millions around the world. Together they had led countless people to Jesus. They had not only adopted their three little girls from China, but they had started a ministry to open doors so that more families could adopt from China. They were generous, giving, loving people.

So why?

>> Digging Deeper

I don't want to mislead you. I don't have a definitive answer to this question. But what I can promise you is that we will take an amazing journey together as we seek to understand God's healing power.

Before exploring Exodus 15, the first place we meet *Jehovah Rapha*—God the Healer, let's read a passage from Exodus 14 to get us acclimated to where we are in the journey of God's people.

Read Exodus 14:15–25. This passage shares one of God's greatest miracles.

> [When the Israelites had reached the other side of the Red Sea, the Lord said to Moses,] "Now take your staff and reach out over the sea. The waters which I parted will crash upon the Egyptians and cover their chariots and chariot-drivers." (Exodus 14:26b)

Moses obeyed, raised his hand and reached out over the sea. In that moment, Scripture says "the walls of water collapsed" (Exodus 14:27b). The Israelites watched as the rushing waters swallowed every chariot, chariot-driver, and the entire Egyptian army.

In a song of celebration following the miracle, the people sang these words: "By the blast of your nostrils the waters piled up. The surging waters stood like a wall; the deep waters congealed in the heart of the sea" (Exodus 15:8 NIV). Moses' use of the word *congealed* tells us the water turned from a liquid to a solid. God blew His breath over the waters and caused them to divide and turn into two walls of ice. Can you imagine? The Israelites walked safely between two walls of water on dry ground. Yet, moments later, they stood in awe as they watched hundreds and hundreds of drowned Egyptian soldiers wash up on shore. God's people were now truly free from their oppressors!

Read Exodus 15:1–19. What did the people do next?

After a time of celebration and praise, Moses led the Israelites away from the Red Sea and into the Desert of Shur to begin their long journey to the Promised Land. This was the very same area where Abraham had lived at one time and where the angel of the Lord had found Hagar when she fled from Sarah.

God's people traveled for three days. First, they lacked for food. God provided. Then they lacked for water—twice. We already read about one time God provided water. Here is another.

Read Exodus 15:22–25. What happened when the Israelites finally found water?

What did the Israelites call that place?

Why had the Lord led them into a waterless wilderness? Then when He did provide water, why was it bitter? Perhaps He was testing them to see if they would trust Him. Perhaps He was punishing them because He discerned the mistrust in their hearts. We can't be sure, but what we do know is that God was there, in their midst, leading them in a cloud by day and in a pillar of fire by night.

The grumbling Israelites turned their anger and frustration toward Moses. And, as he always did when he needed help, Moses cried out to God. And as He always did, the Lord provided—but this time in a most unusual way.

How did God provide? Why do you suppose He chose this method?

Why use a piece of wood? Some theologians propose this piece of wood was a "type" of the cross of Christ, a foreshadowing. Just as the cross sweetens the bitter waters of affliction and brings salvation to all who stand at its foot and believe, the piece of wood sweetened the water, thus satisfying the people's thirst and thereby saving their lives.[3]

In the next few verses, God issues a decree to test His people's faithfulness: "If you will listen closely to My voice—the voice of your God—and do what is right in My eyes, pay attention to My instructions, and keep all of My laws, then I will not bring on you any of the plagues that I did on the Egyptians" (Exodus 15:26). The NIV and the King James use the word *diseases* rather than *plagues*.

Read Exodus 15:26 in your Bible. I purposely left off the final words of verse 26. Write God's last words of his decree below.

God revealed Himself to His people in a name. With that name came a promise. He promised to be the Lord who heals them, but His promise contained a condition.

What was God's condition?

God's condition was clear. Obedience brings blessings. Another way of stating this: blessings *follow* obedience. God gave very specific directions, and the Israelites knew exactly what God expected of them: First, they were to listen carefully to the voice of the Lord. Second, they were to do what is right in His eyes. Third, they were to obey His commands. Fourth, they were to keep all His decrees.

Blessings follow obedience.

After God made this promise, He led them to an oasis—a place of bountiful blessings.

Read Exodus 15:27. What did the Israelites find here?

Read Psalm 19:7–10. Share a few truths you learn about God and His Word from these verses.

In this life we will endure trials; we will experience both the bitter and the sweet. But with God, we can trust there will always be "the sweet." Times of refreshing will come.

In this life we will endure trials; we will experience both the bitter and the sweet. But with God, we can trust there will always be "the sweet." Times of refreshing will come.

🖋 **Read Lamentations 3:22–24.** What do these verses say?

🖋 What did the bitter waters reveal about the hearts of the Israelites?

🖋 In your own life, when bitter times come, how do you respond? What fills your heart?

⟫⟫ Apply It

The bitter waters of Marah were the first of many testing grounds for the Israelites on their long journey to the Promised Land. They failed their first test big time! Only a few days had passed since God's parting of the Red Sea, one of the most majestic and awesome displays of God's power. How could they grumble and complain? Why did they not just pray for another provision, another act of deliverance?

The answer lies in our sin nature. Call it fear. Call it lack of faith. Call it rage. We are weak and fragile creatures. We want our needs met, and we want them met now!

Yet God calls us to trust in Him no matter our circumstances. He gives us His names—*Elohim, El Roi, Jehovah Nissi,* and *Jehovah Rapha*—so that we can *know* Him. Friend, we only trust those we know, and we cannot trust God if we don't know God. I'd like to encourage you by asking you to examine your own heart today.

God calls us to trust in Him no matter our circumstances.

Do you know Him? I mean, do you really know God enough to trust Him as you do your best friend? If not, why not?

What fills your heart today? Do you need refreshing? Share what is on your heart. Then take a moment to ask God to help you to overcome any feelings that may keep you from fully trusting that He has your best interests in mind.

Jehovah Rapha, God *your* Healer, is waiting for you to come to Him with what is on your heart. He wants to bring healing to your circumstances, your relationship, your hurt, your pain. Open His Word so that He can touch your heart with a "piece of wood" ... a piece of the cross ... a piece of His grace-filled heart. And when you read His Word, listen carefully. Do what is right in His eyes. Obey what you hear. When you do these things, His sweet living water will flow into the bitter waters of your heart and bring healing, joy, and everlasting hope.

Part Two: King Hezekiah's Story

Memory Verse: I am the LORD, who heals you.

—Exodus 15:26 (NIV)

Let's dig deeper into Scripture's revelations about God our Healer. Today we meet Hezekiah, king of Judah. Listen to what the author of 2 Kings writes about Hezekiah:

> He did what was right in the eyes of the LORD, just as his father David had done. He removed the high places, smashed the sacred stones and cut down the Asherah poles … Hezekiah trusted in the LORD, the God of Israel. There was no one like him among all the kings of Judah, either before him or after him. He held fast to the LORD and did not cease to follow him; he kept the commands the LORD had given Moses. And the LORD was with him; he was successful in whatever he undertook. (2 Kings 18:3–7 NIV 1984)

Hezekiah's deep trust in the Lord distinguished him from other kings. From where did this trust come? It came from the generations that had gone before him—his great-grandfather (King Uzziah) and grandfather (King Jotham). Scripture characterizes both kings as wise and godly men who brought great prosperity to Judah and did what was right in the eyes of the Lord.

Read 2 Kings 15:32–16:20 if you would like to learn more about King Hezekiah's heritage.

Sadly, goodness skipped a generation. Hezekiah's father, King Ahaz, failed to do what was right in the eyes of the Lord. In fact, Ahaz failed miserably. Rather than walk in the ways of his father and grandfather, Ahaz engaged in detestable activities—offering sacrifices and burning incense to pagan gods. He even offered one of his own sons as a sacrifice. He followed the traditions of the pagan nations surrounding Judah. His poor leadership and lack of respect for his heritage led to one tragedy after another. Ahaz actually shut down God's holy temple so His people had nowhere to worship. In a few short years, the king lost the power, respect, and favor his predecessors had earned.

To put it plainly, Ahaz was a complete failure as a king, father, and leader. Consequently, when Hezekiah arose to the throne, he inherited a broken and shattered nation.

Thankfully, Hezekiah remembered the days of his grandfather, King Jotham. He realized that his nation was in the mess it was because his father had abandoned the ways and laws of the one true God. He committed to regain Judah's sovereignty, rid it of the evil and wicked pagan practices, and bring the people back to God.

Unlike so many leaders of today, Hezekiah chose *first* to please God before addressing his other pressing political and social issues. His first act as king was to purify the temple. After the priests completed the cleansing process, he directed them to reinstitute the offering of sacrifices. Hezekiah ordered the priests to sacrifice a burnt offering on the altar in the presence of all God's people. As the priests offered that first blood offering, the people sang and praised the Lord, and the entire assembly bowed down in worship.

Imagine the joy that must have filled the people's hearts that day. Imagine the joy that must have filled Hezekiah's heart. Even more so, imagine God's pleasure with his chosen king, Hezekiah.

Read 2 Chronicles 29 if you want to read more about this wonderful time in King Hezekiah's reign.

King Hezekiah understood that for his nation to prosper, it had to first reconcile with God.

Do you think this same reasoning holds true today? Do you think the way a nation treats God and His Word has a direct correlation as to how prosperous and successful it is? If you answered yes, give an example.

Read Proverbs 14:34. Write this verse in your own words. What does it mean to you?

King Hezekiah did not stop there.

Read 2 Chronicles 30:1–12. What did the king do next?

In the midst of the king's efforts to restore Judah, Assyria invaded. Initially, Hezekiah panicked. He didn't seek God's will, acted on his own, and made some critical mistakes which allowed Assyria to press in even harder. Feeling the pressure, Hezekiah finally turned to the One he knew would help.

Read 2 Kings 19:10–12.

The king of Assyria, Sennacherib, sent word to Hezekiah and mocked his God: "Hezekiah, king of Judah, *I warn you* not to be fooled by your God, on whom you rely, when He says, 'Jerusalem will not be conquered by Assyria's king'" (2 Kings 19:10). He recounted all the lands the Assyrians had conquered and told Hezekiah not to put his trust in his God because the gods of all the conquered countries before his had failed their people.

When Hezekiah received this message, he did not cower in fear. He did not negotiate. He did not surrender. He boldly took steps to defend Judah.

What was King Hezekiah's first and most important step? (See 2 Kings 19:14–17.)

Read 2 Kings 19:14–19. What did Hezekiah pray?

This is truly one of the most beautiful and eloquent prayers in all of Scripture. The king cries out to the God he knows will deliver his people.

King Hezekiah humbled himself before God. He repented of his mistake of negotiating with the enemy, trying to win the battle in his own strength and power.

Is there a situation in your life in which you are negotiating, trying to win the battle in your own strength? What has this lesson spoken to you about your situation?

Isaiah then sent word to Hezekiah: "This is the message of the Eternal One, Israel's God: 'Because you have come to Me about Assyria's king, Sennacherib, I have heard *every word you have prayed*'" (2 Kings 19:20).

God promised Hezekiah that He would defend Judah in order to preserve it for His own and for the honor of David (2 Kings

19:32–34). That night the angel of the Lord put to death 185,000 Assyrian soldiers. The people awakened the next morning surrounded by the dead bodies of their enemies. The king of Assyria immediately withdrew what was left of his troops and returned to Nineveh, the capital of the Assyrian empire.

Digging Deeper

Why did I give you all this background? Where does God the Healer fit into Hezekiah's story? Well, I'm glad you asked! Stick with me, friends. We find God the Healer in the rest of the story.

Just after the Lord rescued King Hezekiah and his people from the Assyrians, Hezekiah fell deathly ill. The prophet Isaiah gave the king only days to live, speaking these words: *"This is your last chance to make your final preparations because you are not going to recover; you are going to die"* (2 Kings 20:1b). But Hezekiah had other ideas.

Read 2 Kings 20:2. How did King Hezekiah respond to Isaiah's words?

Read 2 Kings 20:3. What did Hezekiah pray?

At the end of his prayer, what did he do? What does this tell you about Hezekiah's heart?

Read James 5:16b. What does James say in this verse? How does this relate to King Hezekiah?

Hezekiah cried out to God, reminding God of his faithfulness, his devotion, and his obedience. The king was not pleading for divine favor because of his own good works. Rather, he knew God's character, and he was appealing to His character ... His never changing, everlasting character.

> *Hezekiah was not pleading for divine favor because of his own good works. Rather, he knew God's character, and he was appealing to His character.*

Read 2 Samuel 22:21–25. This is a portion of David's song of praise after the Lord delivered him from the hands of all his enemies, including Saul. What do David's words teach us about the character of God?

Neither David's words nor King Hezekiah's words are self-righteous and boasting when read in the context of their stories. Both men desired to please the Lord in everything they did as the

Lord's anointed. Both knew God's ways and knew He rewarded those who faithfully served Him.

Obviously, King Hezekiah's heart *and* his prayer brought pleasure to the Lord because just a few verses later, we read these words: "This is the message of the Eternal One, the God of your ancestor David: 'I have listened to your prayer and have witnessed the tears falling down your face; therefore I am going to heal you'" (2 Kings 20:5b).

Read 2 Kings 20:5–6. What specifically did Isaiah tell King Hezekiah about his healing?

How did God heal Hezekiah (verse 7)? Why do you think He used what he did? What lesson(s) can we learn from this?

Think of a time in your own life when you desperately needed God to intervene. How did you approach God in prayer? Did you ask for His help based on your own good works? Or did you rest in and trust His character and His promises?

I wonder if using figs was God's way of showing us that medicine is "of God." God could have performed a miraculous healing as He had done before and would do many times again. But He did not. He chose to use figs. Did God want to teach that His choosing medical means for healing is not evidence of disbelief? And that when a doctor heals using medical means, it's still God at work healing in and through another's hands?

Bible scholars and students have debated Hezekiah's story of healing for years. Should the king have prayed for healing? Was his healing God's *perfect* will or His *permissive* will? Is there a difference? If so, what is the difference between God's *perfect* will and His *permissive* will?

Take a moment to reflect on this question: Is there a difference between God's *perfect* will and His *permissive* will for us? If so, does it really matter?

Just as we sometimes give in to our children when we know it is not what is best for them, I wonder if God does the same for us. Maybe sometimes God answers our prayers, even if it's not His best for us, so that we learn a lesson. Let's examine the remainder of Hezekiah's life to see if we can glean an answer to our question.

> *Maybe sometimes God answers our prayers, even if it's not His best for us, so that we learn a lesson.*

Some argue that Hezekiah got his way, but it was not God's best for him or his people because in those extra fifteen years the Lord granted him, the king made some grave mistakes. He boasted of and showed off his storehouse of treasures to the Babylonian envoys who came to visit him. Isaiah rebuked him for his boasting, warning: "A time is near when everything in your house, including everything that your ancestors have contributed until today, will be taken to Babylon. Not one item will remain in your house" (2 Kings 20:17).

Additionally, after his healing, King Hezekiah had a son, Manasseh, who turned out to be one of Judah's most wicked kings (2 Kings 20:21). Had Hezekiah died, Judah may have been spared the evil reign of that son.

On the other hand, some argue it was God's best because at the time of King Hezekiah's sickness, he had no children. Yet God had promised that Judah would always have a descendant of David on the throne. If Hezekiah had died with no heir, this promise of God would have been broken. Some argue Hezekiah begged for healing so that he could bring forth an heir to the throne, making his prayer not a selfish prayer but a prayer of fulfillment for the entire nation. In fact, Isaiah's language in 2 Kings 20:1 (NKJV) literally means, "Pick out a man to succeed you to the throne." With no heir to succeed him, Hezekiah was simply holding God to His promise.

And although Manasseh was a godless king, his grandson, Josiah, was righteous and continually did what was right in God's eyes, just as David and Hezekiah had done. Had Hezekiah died, there would have been no Josiah.

Here is another interesting fact to note: the Bible indicates that during Hezekiah's last fifteen years of rule, he joined with a group of scribes known as the "men of Hezekiah" (Proverbs 25:1) to write out and put in order the Old Testament Scriptures. One commentator writes that the Hebrew letters "H Z K" appear at the end of many Old Testament books in the Hebrew manuscripts. It would seem that, in gratitude to God for sparing his life, Hezekiah devoted the last fifteen years of his life to ensuring the reliability and readability of God's Word.[4]

⟫ Apply It

What truths can we extract from Hezekiah's story? God has the power to heal, and He often does so in answer to prayer. We know that living a righteous life, like the one Hezekiah lived, gives us the right to appeal to God for favor, blessings, and healing. James 5:16 tells us that the prayer of a righteous man or woman is powerful and effective. But in the end, it's God's decision. He is sovereign. The very fact that He gave Isaiah these words for Hezekiah, "I have heard your prayer … I will heal you," reminds us of that sovereignty (2 Kings 20:5 NIV).

God has the power to heal, and He often does so in answer to prayer.

Read Matthew 6:33. What does it mean to "seek first the kingdom of God"?

What does it mean to seek "His righteousness"?

What are "all these things" that will be given? (See Matthew 6:19–34.)

Friend, God calls us to concern ourselves with the things of God rather than with our physical needs, whether great or small. He doesn't want us to be anxious or to worry. When we center our lives on God, His Word, and His will for our lives, He will supply everything we *need*—not necessarily everything we *want*—in His timing. This is living by faith. When we surrender our circumstances to God, He, through His Spirit, dispenses a fresh filling of faith.

Whether we are walking through the best of times or the worst, God makes it unquestionably clear that we are not to worry. This passage tells us not to worry five times! Five times in nine verses. Do you think God means it? We are not to be concerned about tomorrow. Why? Because each day has enough to keep us busy! God promises to care for our daily needs.

Before falling captive to worry, fear, and doubt, we must turn to *Jehovah Rapha*, the One who is the Healer. And when we come before His throne, we must come boldly and ask in full faith, believing God the Healer will heal. It's His nature. It's His character.

But in our praying, we must acknowledge that He is sovereign. We pray knowing that whatever the end result, His plan is best— even when we cannot see it with our eyes or feel it with our hearts. Sometimes God chooses to heal in this earthly life, as in the story of Hezekiah. Sometimes He chooses to heal and restore to wholeness in heaven, as in the story of little Maria Chapman. But this should not change how we pray. We should always pray in full faith, knowing that He has our best interests in mind.

We pray knowing that whatever the end result, His plan is best— even when we cannot see it with our eyes or feel it with our hearts.

Let's close our time together with Mary Beth Chapman's final words in *Choosing to See:*

> We ... got a copy of Maria's birth name in its Chinese characters and brought the paper to her Chinese friend.
>
> "Ah, I see," her friend said. "This is very similar, but more specific. The name means spring river!"
>
> We found that name to be even more significant. A spring river results from the melting away of winter's snow. The purest water flows from spring rivers. God's means by which formerly frozen ground can soften and bloom again with the life of spring.
>
> So God confirmed this truth yet again: I can choose to SEE His story, or I can miss it. And I know—in the winter of our grieving and the frozen mourning of my plans that will never be and my dreams that have died—the reality is this: God's warm breath is on the move. New life is budding ... and often where I expected it the least, like right inside of me.[5]

Yes, as with the Chapmans, there will be times when God doesn't do things the way we'd like. Times when He is silent. It's in these times we must *know* God intimately. Knowing Him intimately means we know and understand the breadth of His healing power—that it extends beyond the physical to spiritual and emotional healing. We can walk confidently through anything, even seemingly unanswered healing prayers.

My friend, I want you to know that God ministers to us most in our places of doubt, questioning, grief, and suffering. He takes us to deep places that otherwise we could not go because we are desperate. Deep faith, abiding faith carries us through these most difficult and confusing times. Yes, God heals the physical. But when physical healing doesn't come, His healing reaches beyond to heal our broken hearts and broken dreams.

Do you have a broken dream today? Have you lost someone you love? Do you or someone you love suffer with a chronic illness for which there is no known cure? If you're experiencing something like this in your life right now, take a few minutes to write out a prayer asking God to help you trust Him in the midst of your circumstances.

Sweet friend, God knows your heart. He knows your pain. He is *enough*. He alone is the One who can bring healing and wholeness to your heart. And He will—in His time and in His way. Come to *Jehovah Rapha*. He is waiting.

God knows your heart. He knows your pain. He is enough.

159

Part Three:
God's Will for Healing

> **Memory Verse:** I am the LORD, who heals you.
>
> —Exodus 15:26 (NIV)

How are you coming along with your memory verses? You have some verses tucked deeply in your heart, I know. I'm so proud of you! I pray that when you need to call on these attributes of God or share them with a friend, they will roll off your tongue because you have faithfully and obediently committed them to memory.

What is God's will for healing? Before we can steadfastly believe God for healing, we must understand two things. First, we must know *what* His Word teaches about healing. And second, we must know *how* to pray for that healing.

Our two previous stories provided great examples of God's healing power and how that power has worked in the lives of His people. But now we'll examine what God's Word specifically says about His will on this matter of healing.

The word *healer* in the Old Testament is a translation of the Hebrew word *Rapha*, which means "to mend, to cure, to heal, to thoroughly make whole," and it refers to God alone as the One doing the healing.[6]

Proverbs 4:20–22 has always been one of my favorite passages on healing because God gives us very clear instructions there.

Read Proverbs 4:20–22. What are God's instructions?

First, we must *hear* the Word. Sometimes that means listening to a sermon. Sometimes it's listening to worship music. Sometimes it's opening God's Word and reading, praying for Him to give you "ears to hear" what you are reading. And sometimes it's quieting ourselves enough to hear His still, small voice.

Second, we must *receive* the Word. This entails inviting God into the process, asking Him to open our hearts to take in the truths He gives us.

Finally, we must allow the Word to *penetrate* our hearts. Once we open our ears to hear it and our hearts to receive it, we must pray that it will lodge deeply within. God's Spirit must stir up the soil of our hearts so that His Word takes root. It's only when it takes root that He can use it for His purposes—to teach, rebuke, correct, and train us in righteousness (2 Timothy 3:16). We must be willing to allow God's Word to penetrate even to those shadowy spaces and deep crevices we hide from the rest of the world.

God's Spirit must stir up the soil of our hearts so that His Word takes root.

Following these steps opens the pathway for God's truths and promises to travel into our hearts and breathe life and healing to our whole body!

Digging Deeper

Years ago, a routine visit to my doctor revealed that I had elevated blood pressure. My heart sank. I was only in my thirties with two little children. I had witnessed the difficulties my other family members had with high blood pressure, and I didn't want to join their ranks.

Thankfully, it was not high enough to require drastic action, but my doctor did prescribe a low-dose blood pressure medication. I took the medication faithfully. Unfortunately, it did not markedly affect my blood pressure.

During this same time, I began praying fervently for healing. I asked specifically for the Lord to lower my blood pressure and for wisdom to know the role I needed to play to bring about that healing. God led me to examine my lifestyle—my diet, my activity level, and my stress level. Surprise, surprise! I was not eating as well as I should. I was not exercising at all, and I certainly could have handled stress better. Determined to correct the problem, I instituted immediate changes. I changed my diet. I added an exercise regimen. And most importantly, I initiated a quiet time, something that I had done in the past but had stopped making time for on a regular basis.

As part of this quiet time, I memorized Scriptures on healing. I claimed God's promise from Proverbs 4:22—that His Word is life and health to my body. I literally prescribed myself an additional medication—God's Word. I ingested it every day, just as I did the blood pressure medicine, believing in full faith that God would heal my body of whatever was causing my hypertension.

Within a few months, my blood pressure came down. With my doctor's permission, I stopped my medicine and continued my regimen of a healthy diet, exercise, and "taking" God's Word as my daily medicine. My blood pressure not only continued to decrease, but praise God, it has remained low to this day. Yes, high blood pressure is in my genes. But I also love and serve a God who is able to trump genetics!

God taught me a powerful truth during that time: He is my Healer, and His Word is my daily medicine! As I delved deeper into the subject of God's healing, my studies led me to Isaiah 53:5. Before we study this verse, let's read Isaiah 53 in its entirety.

Read Isaiah 53. Who is the "Servant"?

Isaiah's words are so important. Seven hundred years *before* Christ appeared, Isaiah prophesied not only Christ's coming but also what His coming would mean for God's people! If we don't read God's Word cover to cover, beginning to end, we miss truths like this—truths that gird up our faith and vastly increase our knowledge of the Word and its veracity.

Read Isaiah 53:1–3. How does Isaiah describe the Servant?

Read Isaiah 53:4–6. What does Isaiah teach us in this passage about our Savior?

Isaiah speaks of the Servant being led like a lamb to slaughter, dying for the rebellion of God's people. There is much debate about what exactly the Servant's death "covered." Healing, yes, but is it only inner (spiritual) healing? Or does it extend to outer (physical) healing as well? Scholars cannot agree, but let's stretch our brains, go before the Lord, and ask Him for wisdom and discernment as we search His Word together.

Isaiah 53:4 says, "[Jesus] took up our *pain* and bore our *suffering* (NIV, emphasis added)." The King James says, "[Jesus] hath borne our *griefs,* and carried our *sorrows"* (emphasis added). The issue confronting us is what do the words *pain, suffering, griefs,* and *sorrows* encompass?

Griefs translates from the Hebrew word *choliy,* which means "sickness and disease." *Sorrows* translates from the Hebrew word *makob,* which means "affliction and pain." These words alone do not make clear whether Jesus' death is limited to spiritual healing or extends to physical healing as well.[7] But Jesus' disciple Matthew gives us his insight into Isaiah 53:4 in Matthew 8:16–17.

Read Matthew 8:16–17.

Just after Jesus "drove out the spirits with a word and healed all the sick" (NIV), Matthew writes the following words: "This was to fulfill what was spoken through the Prophet Isaiah: 'He took up our infirmities and bore our diseases'" (NIV). Matthew's use of the words *sick* and *disease* here implies someone physically sick with "a malady, a disease," thereby confirming the notion that the fourth verse of Isaiah may refer to both physical and spiritual healing.[8]

What we do know for a fact from Isaiah's words is that by dying on the cross, Jesus took on our sickness and disease. He bore them in His own perfect body, a body free of sin, sickness, and disease. I don't want us to ever forget what a heavy load this was for our sinless Savior. But He carried it because He loved us so much.

God is our Healer. He sent His only Son to die on the cross for our healing. That healing comes first in the form of spiritual healing, the forgiveness of sins. Because of Jesus, sin and death no longer bind us. We have become children of God who can walk confidently in the righteousness of Christ with the hope and promise of everlasting life!

But Jesus also died for physical healing. God healed spiritually *and* physically in the Old Testament. Jesus healed spiritually *and* physically in the New Testament. God's Word clearly teaches that His character never changes. He is the same yesterday, today, and forever (Hebrews 13:8). Therefore, you and I can conclude with full assurance that we are to pray for physical healing.

But we must temper our healing prayers by keeping God's purpose for prayer foremost in our minds. And that purpose is *not* to ask for and get what we want. Although that is certainly a part of prayer's purpose, it's viewing prayer solely from our human perspective.

There is another perspective—God's. God calls us to Himself so that we can know Him more. God created us for relationship. He desires to communicate with us. Prayer opens the door for that communication.

Read Luke 18:1; Colossians 4:2; and 1 Thessalonians 5:17. What do these verses teach us about prayer?

The challenge in prayer comes when we marry our prayer for healing with the unchanging character of God the Healer, and then the healing never comes in this lifetime.

How can that happen?

Why would God teach us to pray for healing if He knows that in certain circumstances it will never come in this lifetime?

Why? Because prayer is not about the answer! It's about God. Let me say that again. Prayer is not about the answer. It's about God.

Prayer is not about the answer. It's about God.

I want to share five biblical steps that have helped me pray more effectively, especially when praying for healing. I encourage you to try these prayer steps when you go to God in prayer.

- Tell God your need. (Philippians 4:6)

- Pray and ask in full faith without doubting. (James 1:6)

- Commit what you have asked to God's sovereignty. (Isaiah 46:9–10)

- Leave your request with Him to act according to His perfect will. (Psalm 57:1–2; Isaiah 55:9)

- Trust that His answer is the best way to accomplish His plan and purpose. (Proverbs 3:5–6)

Praying in accordance with these principles ensures that we pray as Jesus did in the garden of Gethsemane: "not my will, but yours be done" (Luke 22:42 NIV).

Oh friend, I know how difficult it is to surrender to God's will. Even Jesus had to surrender His will to God the Father. But we have a God who loves us unconditionally (Psalm 136:26). A God who promises He knows the plans He has for us, plans to prosper and not to harm, plans to give us hope and a future (Jeremiah 29:11). A God who sacrificed His only Son for us (John 3:16). A God who has opened heaven's gates for us so we can spend eternity with Him (John 14:2).

Seemingly unanswered prayer threatens to weaken our faith and trust in God, and sometimes that leads to discouragement or even despair. The result: We give up on prayer and God. But by following this five-step process and standing on the character and promises of God, we head off that discouragement and despair. We prepare our hearts and minds for however God answers. Why? Because the last three steps enable us to trust God. We trust Him to answer in the way He sees fit—the way that He knows is best for us.

This does not mean that when we don't get what we want, when we want it, we give up. We should not give up on our heart's desire. We should pray and wait, wait and pray. We should persevere. We should scour God's Word for promises that speak to our heart's cry. We should cling to our prayer. We should pray without doubting. We should wait expectantly. This is all part of the process. It deepens our faith in ways nothing else can.

But at some point, we need to reconcile our prayers with God's sovereignty. God gave me a most beautiful example of how this is done. At a recent speaking event, I met a lovely young woman who longed to be a mother. She and her husband had been trying for several years to conceive, to no avail. All of her siblings and cousins were having children. She had sixteen nieces and nephews. My heart went out to her, and I offered to pray for her. I told her that I would pray for God to give her the desire of her heart. Just as those words rolled off my tongue, she interrupted and spoke these most amazing faith-filled words: "And if it's not God's will for us to have our own baby, Wendy, will you pray for God to change the desire of my heart?" That, my friend, is surrendered faith!

At some point, we need to reconcile our prayers with God's sovereignty.

Eventually, God will answer. And that is when we trust Him unequivocally, no matter what we hear. He may give us the desire of our heart. He may change the desire of our heart. He may also redirect our prayers.

Paul's life provides us another poignant example of how God answers healing prayer. Paul asked—no, begged—God to take away what the Bible called a "thorn in his flesh." Paul laid his heart on the line with God when he pleaded with God to remove his thorn, not once, but three times!

Did God not answer Paul's prayer? Yes, he answered it, but not in the way Paul asked. God answered Paul's prayer this way: "My grace is all you need. My power works best in weakness" (2 Corinthians 12:9 NLT). God did not remove Paul's thorn; He gave him the grace to bear it.

God speaks of prayer often. And if we read His Word carefully, He always qualifies His promises concerning prayer.

🖋 **Read John 14:13–14; 15:7; 16:23–24; and 1 John 5:14.** Write down what you learn from these verses about prayer.

To ask in Jesus' name is to ask with the same attitude as Jesus when He prayed to His Father. Jesus prayed only to do His Father's will.

> To ask in Jesus' name is to ask with the same attitude as Jesus when He prayed to His Father. Jesus prayed only to do His Father's will.

Read Matthew 6:10 and Luke 22:42. List several examples of Jesus praying according to His Father's will.

Apply It

Friends, please don't consider this an exhaustive explanation of the sovereignty of God and how it relates to prayer. My simple desire is to help you to find a deeper understanding of healing prayer and how it intersects with God's sovereignty. What I can tell you with great certainty is that every prayer offered in faith, with Christ's attitude of humility, will be answered. And we can know and trust that the answer will be for our best.

I know I often fall short of praying this kind of prayer. Instead, I tell God what I want and what He ought to do. I politely demand my own way. But that is my flesh praying—my old nature. When I am led by my Spirit—my new nature—I pray differently. I pray in the authority of my new standing as a child of God. I pray confidently, but with a submissive heart for what I need. I pray God's Word and wait expectantly. And when the answer looks different than what I asked, I trust in God's sovereignty. I pray for Him to change the desire of my heart. I surrender my will to His and pray for the strength to walk in obedience to His answer.

As we yearn to go deeper in prayer and understand God's role in healing prayer, let us pray as one of Jesus' disciples prayed in Luke 11:1.

Read Luke 11:1. Write the disciple's simple, yet humble, prayer below.

Is there a prayer with which you are struggling? A prayer for healing? A prayer for restoration or reconciliation? A prayer for financial provision? How have you been praying? Honestly examine your heart based on what we have learned. If you find that you have not been praying in accordance with the biblical principles we learned today, rewrite your prayer and invite God to work in a fresh, new way through your obedient, submissive heart.

Part Four:
The Healing Power of Jesus

Memory Verse: I am the LORD, who heals you.

—Exodus 15:26 (NIV)

The New Testament pages are filled with incredible stories recounting Jesus' miraculous healings. Choosing which ones to share is quite a challenge, because each one contains its own unique lesson. But choose I must, so let's begin.

However, before we jump into the stories themselves, let's travel back with Luke to the time Jesus met Satan in the wilderness. Jesus' temptation came not long after John the Baptist baptized Him.

Read Matthew 3:13–17 and Luke 3:21–22. Share what happens in these two passages.

This is a pivotal point in the life of Christ. At age thirty, the time had arrived for Jesus to embark on the ministry for which God had sent Him. His Father called Him to leave His private life and thrust Him into public ministry.

Read Luke 4:1–2. What happened to Jesus just after He was baptized?

Why do you think God led Christ into the wilderness immediately after His baptism?

Have you ever received an invitation to join a group that required an initiation activity of some kind? I have, and I will never forget it. I pledged a sorority in college. On our last day of pledge week, some of the senior members "kidnapped" our pledge class, blindfolded us, and took us to a secluded location. They removed our blindfolds and left us alone to find our way back. Frightening? Yes. Team-building? Yes. Being left alone in that strange place caused my fellow pledges and me to work together. We helped one another and encouraged one another, most especially me because I was terrified—they dropped us off in a graveyard! But we did it. We completed our pledgeship with that initiation. The next day, we became full-fledged members of our sorority.

Perhaps God wanted to give His Son the opportunity to handle some tailor-made temptations before stepping into His public ministry where He would face seemingly insurmountable challenges and temptations. Perhaps God wanted to set some ground rules with Satan about God's "authority" on earth before the battle for our souls began. What an intense season of temptation God allowed when He permitted Satan to engage His Son this way.

Read Luke 4:3–12. List the three specific temptations Jesus faced.

When faced with the first temptation, Jesus had not eaten for forty days. Because He was both human as well as divine, we can be certain He was hungry. If He wasn't, Satan would not have tempted

Jesus with food. Jesus' divine nature could have easily turned a stone into bread.

How had God provided? (See Luke 3:21–22; 4:1.)

God prepared Jesus in advance. And He does the same for us!

Read 1 Corinthians 10:13. Share how God prepares us.

How did Jesus respond?

Read Luke 4:4. What was Jesus' response? Whom did He quote?

Jesus ensured Satan understood that His Father's Word trumped Satan's word—every time! This is a truth you and I must never forget! When Satan tries to sow seeds of doubt in your heart and mind, speak the truth of God's Word to him every time, no matter the circumstance.

In the second temptation, Satan revealed to Jesus all the kingdoms of the world and said he would give Jesus authority over them—because he had authority over them—if Jesus would worship him.

✒ **Read Luke 4:8.** What was Jesus' response? Whom did He quote?

Satan then issued his third and final temptation. He took Jesus to the highest point of the temple and said, "Since You're the Son of God, just jump. Just throw Yourself into the air" (Luke 4:9). Satan then followed his temptation by *quoting Scripture*! In verse 10, Satan actually quoted God's Word.

Friend, don't miss this: Satan quoted God's Word. He knows the Bible, and he won't hesitate to twist it for his purposes at every opportunity.

> *Friend, don't miss this: Satan quoted God's Word. He knows the Bible, and he won't hesitate to twist it for his purposes at every opportunity.*

✒ **Read Luke 4:12.** What was Jesus' response? Whom did He quote?

Satan's intent here was to tempt the Son to test the Father. What a desperate and foolish creature. But Jesus withstood the test. In fact, Jesus used the opportunity to *clarify* the issue of authority. Yes, Satan has temporary power on this earth, but Jesus has authority over all of heaven, on the earth, and under the earth!

🖋 **Read Colossians 1:15–20.** How does this passage settle the issue of Jesus' authority?

Satan executed an all-out assault against Jesus, His position as Messiah, and His identity as the Son of God. God sent Jesus to earth in human form so that He could identify with our sins and temptations. He endured temptation so that He could identify with our humanness and demonstrate His sinless character. When we are tempted, let's remember this trying time in the life of our Savior.

God the Father had just identified Jesus in Luke 3: "You are my Son, the Son I love, and in You I take great pleasure" (Luke 3:22). Here we find Jesus just one chapter later being tempted by Satan. Temptation does not mean we are weak or that God is displeased with us. Rather, when we are tempted, we need to look for God's purposes. It may be God is giving us the opportunity to stand strong on His promises, as Jesus did. It might be a time to remember *who* we are and *whose* we are. It may be our time to be identified as His child in whom He is well pleased!

When we are tempted, we need to look for God's purposes. It may be God is giving us the opportunity to stand strong on His promises, as Jesus did.

But be warned, temptation is not a one-time occurrence. Satan came after Jesus three times, each time more aggressively than the time before. Don't be deceived. Satan is relentless.

Jesus overcame each temptation with just a few powerful, Holy Spirit-filled words. He spoke the Word of God, the most powerful weapon we have to combat the evil one.

Digging Deeper

Are you a bit curious about why we began with Jesus in the wilderness?

 Read Luke 4:14. What happened just after the time of temptation?

These words are incredibly significant to the rest of our chapter as we meet Jesus, the Great Physician. So don't miss this! God led Jesus into the wilderness full of His *Spirit*. Jesus came out of the wilderness full of the Spirit's *power*!

Read that statement one more time: God led Jesus into the wilderness full of God's *Spirit*. Jesus came out of the wilderness full of God's *power*.

Jesus did not come out the other side of temptation weak and exhausted. No! He came out anointed and empowered to do the work for which God had called Him. And not only did He come out empowered to do ministry, He immediately announced His anointing and calling to the people in the synagogue in His hometown of Nazareth.

Jesus did not come out the other side of temptation weak and exhausted. No! He came out anointed and empowered to do the work for which God had called Him.

Read Luke 4:18–19. Jesus basically gives His job description. Write down at least four specific purposes for which God sent Jesus to earth. From where did these words come?

Now read Luke 4:21. After Jesus read these words, what did He say to the people in the synagogue?

Jesus announced to everyone present and to everyone who has ever heard or read those words that He is *the* Messiah. He is God's *chosen* instrument to once and for all free God's people from the bonds of sin and death.

Luke 4:31–37 recounts one of Christ's first miraculous healings. At Jesus' spoken word, a demon "came out" of a possessed man. But this was only the beginning of Jesus' healing ministry.

How I wish we could study every one of Jesus' healings. Each one teaches great and compelling lessons. My prayer is that the stories we have chosen are the best ones for our purposes—understanding the character of God and how that character intersects with our daily lives.

Now let's turn to Luke 5, specifically verses 12–15, and to the story of a devastating disease: leprosy. The word alone instilled a sense of fear and loathing in ancient times, and still does even today in some parts of the world. In biblical times, leprosy referred to a series of skin conditions that disfigured and destroyed the human body. It was so common during Old Testament times that God gave Moses specific instructions on how to deal with people who contracted the disease. The law identified lepers as not only physically sick but also religiously and ceremonially unclean. Consequently, it required that they be isolated from the community, outside the cities, away from their friends and loved ones. Mosaic law stated that no ceremonially clean person could even touch a leper. So not only were lepers denied fellowship and social interaction, they were denied love and affection as well. If someone did come in contact with a leper, he or she immediately became ceremonially unclean. All of this comes into play in the scene that is about to unfold.

How did the leper approach Jesus (verse 12)? What does this say about his heart?

Why do you suppose the leper said, "If you are willing" (Luke 5:12 NIV)?

Luke beautifully portrays the humility of this leper as he bowed before Jesus and called Him "Lord." He believed Jesus could heal him. It was not a matter of could; it was a matter of would. *Would Jesus be willing?* The leper knew Jesus was able, but he doubted whether he would actually do it for him; he doubted whether he was worthy.

How often do we speak those same words? We ask something of Jesus that we know He can do, but we wonder if we are worthy—if He would really be willing to do such a thing for us. We focus on our sin, and how we disappoint Jesus time and time again, rather than on the One who forgives our sin.

Tucked inside the leper's words is really the question: *Is my healing part of Your purpose and plan?* We know God has a plan for us. Scripture teaches this in Jeremiah 29:11. He had a plan for this leper. But did that plan involve healing? The answer is a resounding yes! With compassion, Jesus reached out and touched this unclean man and spoke these words, "I am willing ... Be healed" (Luke 5:13a NLT).

Did you see what Jesus did? He didn't just speak healing words. Jesus touched him. Jesus touched the untouchable—a man no one else would touch. He reached out and restored him to wholeness. Jesus did not need to touch the leper to heal him, because by His very Word He could heal. He touched this leper to meet a deeper need, his need for love and affection. Jesus' touch healed the man's heart, and His Word healed the man's disease.

Do you have a rotting place in your life you cannot share with another single soul? A place of shame? Guilt? Unforgiveness? Addiction? Bitterness? Prejudice? We all have that place, a place so ugly that if others knew of it, they might reject us or judge us. But we need not be afraid. In Jesus, we have access to the very same source of cleansing as the leper did. He is waiting for us to come to Him. We need only humble our hearts and bow before Him, not only voicing our request, but also seeking *His* purpose for our lives and not our own. And again, we must recognize in that seeking, there are times when God may not heal in the way we expected.

As I've previously mentioned, this is one of the most difficult aspects of Christianity for me to understand and accept. Why does God sometimes heal in this lifetime and sometimes decide to heal only in heaven? The only solace I find is in the fact that I trust *who* God is. And I pray that through our time together, as we learn more about the character of our God, we are learning to trust Him more and more with the turn of every page.

God is sovereign. Every decision He makes is intentional. He sees the "big picture" that we cannot.

> *God is sovereign. Every decision He makes is intentional. He sees the "big picture" that we cannot.*

This story and the passage of Scripture ends with the words, "Immediately the man is cured" (Luke 5:13b).

What might you have felt if you were the leper? What would you have done?

Can you imagine the overwhelming sense of gratitude and freedom that filled the leper's heart? Jesus' touch and spoken word gave him physical healing and new life.

Just a few verses later, we find Jesus teaching His disciples, the Pharisees, and the teachers of the law.

🖋 **Read Luke 5:17–26.** Write down the last sentence of verse 17.

🖋 What do these words mean?

🖋 Do you think they mean that there are times when Jesus lacked the power to heal? Why or why not?

One of the reasons I love to teach the Word of God is because I love to explore challenging passages. This one challenges me, and I want us to think about it together.

To discover answers to questions like this—whether Jesus lacked the power to heal at certain times—it helps to go to one of the original languages of the Gospel writers. Luke tells us the "healing power of the Lord was with Him" (Luke 5:17a). The Greek word for *power* used here is *dunamis*, meaning "power, miracle" and almost always points to "new and higher forces that have entered and are working in this lower world of ours." *Dunamis* refers to God's earthly application of His divine power. He applies His *dunamis* to do a miraculous work on earth to accomplish His heavenly purposes.[9]

God the Father filled God the Son with His divine power, thereby enabling Him to apply that divine power to accomplish His Father's heavenly purposes. So the real issue is whether Jesus was *willing* to use it in these circumstances, and He was.

 **Read Luke 5:18–19.** What happens next in Luke's account?

Imagine this scene with me. Jesus is teaching when, all of a sudden, the ceiling falls in, showering pieces of tile and dirt onto the crowd gathered below. In front of a distinguished audience, comprised of holy men and teachers of the law, a dirty, unkempt man on a mat appears out of nowhere and lands right at Jesus' feet! Because the culture considered the lame and paralyzed outcasts and labeled them as "unclean," the disabled man was not welcome there.

 How did Jesus respond? (See Luke 5:20.)

Jesus' words probably confused the man's friends. They brought him to Jesus because they believed Jesus could heal his legs and make him walk again. And verse 20 tells us that Jesus acted in response to their faith. But Jesus speaks some strange and unexpected words in response to that faith. Rather than just healing him, Jesus' first words to the paralyzed man were, "My friend, all your sins are forgiven" (Luke 5:20b).

Does this statement imply that all sickness results from our sin? We can jump over to the gospel of John to find our answer.

 **Read John 9:1–3.** What happened here?

According to Jesus, why was this man born blind?

Yes, sickness and sin can be connected, but not in the way the early Jews believed. They attributed sickness to sin. If a person was sick, it was either because he sinned or his parents sinned.

In this passage, Jesus did not give the disciples the answer they expected. Finding fault was not important to Him. God created us for His purposes and for His glory. Trials, suffering, and sicknesses come into our lives for very different and distinct reasons. But God always intends for the end result to bring about His purposes and His glory.

So what is the connection between sin and sickness? We live in a fallen world. Our problems, whether physical, emotional, or spiritual, stem from Adam and Eve's disobedience in the garden of Eden. There are times when Jesus connects His healing with forgiveness of sin and other times when He does not. So we can conclude that sometimes sin is an issue in sickness and sometimes it is not.

But *when* is it an issue? That is the question our seeking hearts must ask. I lived for years crippled by fear. It led to periods of sleeplessness, headaches, a racing heart rate, and panic attacks that resulted in several trips to the emergency room. My sin—fear—brought about physical sickness. When God freed me from that fear, it arrested all my physical symptoms. Coincidence? I think not. I confessed my stronghold of fear to God, recognized it as not from Him, and surrendered every bit of it. God forgave my sin, and my physical symptoms disappeared. So you see, sin and sickness can be connected. But not always.

When we are sick, the key for you and me is this: go before the Lord and seek His wisdom regarding our sickness.

⟫ Apply It

As we close this section, note Jesus' last words to the paralyzed man: "I say, get up, take up your mat, and go home" (Luke 5:24b). Moments before, he had said to those gathered, "Just so you'll know that the Son of Man is fully authorized to forgive sins on earth" (Luke 5:24a). Jesus did what He did, in the way in which He did it, so that all present would know the depth and breadth of His authority on this earth.

Friend, sin is a common problem for us all. We sin every day. Some days our sins are few, and other days they are many. Some days they are small, and other days they loom over us like a dark shadow. Alone, we are powerless to overcome our sin. We have one hope and one answer—Jesus.

Is something holding you captive? Unforgiveness? Addiction? Fear? Revenge? People pleasing? If there is, recognize it, confess it, surrender it, and invite God to heal your heart, mind, and soul! He will be faithful to bring healing and freedom to you, as He did to me. Take a few minutes to write a prayer to God sharing the cry of your heart.

Part Five:
Amazing Faith

> **Memory Verse:** I am the LORD, who heals you.
>
> —Exodus 15:26 (NIV)

Amazing faith. Who has it? What is it? In Luke 7, Jesus defines amazing faith for us.

After Jesus' famous Sermon on the Mount, He traveled to the city of Capernaum. It was here that Jesus performed many of His miracles. Luke 7 opens with one such miracle involving a Roman soldier. Luke never reveals his name; all we know is that he served as a centurion in the Roman army, meaning he commanded a century—a group of one hundred soldiers.

Traditionally, Jews hated the Roman soldiers, but that was not the case with this man. They dearly loved and respected him. Why? Because, although a Roman and a Gentile (non-Jew), this centurion lived his life differently than most other soldiers. He treated people kindly and fairly; he valued and respected them and helped build their local synagogue.

At some point, the soldier's servant became gravely ill. The centurion had heard of Jesus and His miraculous powers, so he sent for Jesus to come and heal his ailing servant. The elders immediately went to Jesus and pleaded with Him on the centurion's behalf.

Read Luke 7:4–5. What did the elders say to Jesus?

🖋 What was Jesus' response? (See verse 6.)

🖋 What do you think Jesus heard about this man from the elders that made Him respond as He did?

⟫ Digging Deeper

One thing we must not miss is the value the centurion placed on his servant. In biblical times, slaves had monetary but little human value. If one became weak or ill, most owners would discard them and buy another. But not this centurion. Scripture says this servant's master "highly valued" him. These words translate from the Greek word *entimos*, meaning "held in honor … precious, dear."[10] The centurion held his servant dear to his heart. He valued the one who had spent his life serving him. What a reflection of godly character!

It's interesting to me that throughout the New Testament, Jesus calls us both His servants and His friends. I wonder if the centurion felt the same way toward his servant. Perhaps the servant had become a trusted friend as well. Whatever the case, let's not forget that our Master, too, highly values His servants—you and me. We are precious in His sight. Just as the centurion valued his servant, Christ values us!

Read Luke 7:6–8. Write down three things that stand out to you in the centurion's words for Jesus.

The centurion's story teaches us three lessons about what Jesus values in a servant. First, Jesus values strong character.

What words and actions reveal the centurion's good character?

While good works do not merit God answering our prayers, we must always remember that good works are evidence of God's activity in our lives. They are the fruit that reveal He is at work in us. Abundant fruit reveals good character. And God's favor shines on those who serve others and walk in His ways.

Second, Jesus values humility.

What words reveal the soldier's humility? (See verse 7.)

It appears the centurion had second thoughts about calling for Jesus, so he sent Jesus a message stating that he was not "worthy" to have Him come under his roof. Interestingly, this is the same Greek word John the Baptist spoke in Matthew 3:11, when he said, "I am not fit" to carry Jesus' sandals. The centurion's words reflected not only his high regard for Jesus but also his humility when he considered being in the presence of the Lord.

What happened next models extraordinary faith. Despite his apprehension, the centurion made another request for his servant's healing. He knew Jesus' heart well enough to know that He would respond. He had observed Jesus making Himself available to all types of people who came to Him for healing.

Third, Jesus values the spoken word.

🖋 Write the words the centurion speaks in Luke 7:7b.

I wonder if what Jesus heard between the lines of the centurion's words went something like this: *I am who I am, and people under my authority do what I say. And because You are who You are, if You speak a word, it will be done.* Even if the centurion didn't understand everything about Jesus, he did have a clear understanding of His authority. He knew that what Jesus commanded, He accomplished. Jesus was a man of His word.

Now let's take a look at how Jesus responded when He heard the centurion's words.

🖋 **Read Luke 7:9.** When Jesus turned to the crowd, what did He say?

Amazed translated in the Greek is *thaumazo*, meaning "to wonder, marvel, admire."[11] I don't often think of Jesus being amazed, especially at me. How can the God of the universe be amazed by anything we do? He knows what we will do and say even before we do. So how can we amaze Him?

God cares for us; He values us. Isaiah 66:2 says, "Everything is the product of My hand—*My being and My doing*—that's how all *you see* came to be; *I made it all*. Nevertheless, I am interested in and concerned about even just one person who is humble and downhearted and trembles at my word." God shines His favor on those who are humble, who have contrite hearts, who fear and revere Him and His Word.

God shines His favor on those who are humble, who have contrite hearts, who fear and revere Him and His Word.

One of my favorite verses from Zephaniah says:

> For the LORD your God is living among you.
>   He is a mighty savior.
> He will take delight in you with gladness.
>   With his love, he will calm all your fears
>   He will rejoice over you with joyful songs.
>   (Zephaniah 3:17 NLT)

We are God's workmanship, created with free will to *choose* to say yes to Him. But because of our sin nature, He knows we are prone to say no, to walk in selfish, self-centered, prideful ways. So, He delights in the times when we *choose* obedience, *choose* honor, *choose* to walk in His ways. He esteems such children and shines His favor upon them.

We see this truth come alive in the last verse of the Luke 7 passage. Jesus never stepped foot into the centurion's house. Yet the Roman soldier witnessed the incomparable healing power of Jesus Christ when his weak and dying servant sat up in his bed, fully recovered from his sickness. Don't you wonder what the centurion felt in that moment? What would you have felt?

Oh, how I want to be a woman whose faith amazes God! What about you?

We end our time together in Luke 8. We encounter Jesus just as a man named Jairus, a ruler of the synagogue, fell at His feet begging Him to heal his daughter. Jesus agreed and began the trek to Jairus' house.

While on the way, crowds pressed into Jesus, nearly crushing Him. Have you ever been in that place? My daughter attends the University of Georgia. Several times a year we traveled to Athens for a football game. One hot, sticky Saturday afternoon, we joined the swarms of people herding into the stadium for the sold-out Georgia–South Carolina game. As people pressed in on every side, I felt as if I couldn't breathe. I imagine this crowd sensation to be similar to the one in which Jesus found Himself.

In the midst of the crowd, a woman came up *behind* Him and touched the hem of His robe. Keep two things in mind as you read this story. First, Jesus could not see the woman. Second, she never touched His skin. Yet in that instant, Jesus asked, "Who touched me?" (Luke 8:45).

Everyone denied touching Him. Peter rationalized that Jesus was feeling the crowd pressing against Him. It was as if they thought they would be reprimanded if they said, "Yes, we touched You."

But Jesus repeated His question. And we can gather from His next words that this was not just any touch: "*I felt something*. I felt power going out from Me. I know that somebody touched Me" (Luke 8:46).

The woman sought healing. Luke's and Mark's gospels reveal that this woman had been bleeding for twelve years. She watched her finances dwindle away as each and every doctor failed her. To add to her grief, anyone in that time and place who suffered from bleeding was treated the same as a leper, unclean and isolated from society. She was truly desperate.

As the woman approached Jesus, she thought, "Even if all I touch are His clothes, I know I will be healed" (Mark 5:28). And that is exactly what happened. Immediately upon touching Jesus' cloak, her bleeding stopped.

Jesus knew the touch had released His healing power, and He wanted to identify the one who received it. But why did He want her identity revealed? Perhaps He wanted the woman to declare her faith publicly. Perhaps He wanted others to see her and know of her faith and her healing. Whatever the reason, the healed woman eventually pushed forward, trembling, fell at Jesus' feet, and confessed.

Jesus' then spoke these words: "Daughter, you are well because you *dared* to believe. Go in peace, and stay well" (Mark 5:34b). The King James Version says, "Daughter, be of good comfort: thy faith hath made thee whole; go in peace." *Whole* as used here can refer to both physical and spiritual healing.

Jesus did not want this woman to see herself as a pitiful soul who begged and got what she asked. He wanted her to leave confident in who she was as a child of God—a woman whose unwavering faith brought her perfect healing and peace.

Apply It

Let the truth of who Jesus is sink deep into the marrow of your bones. Our Lord and Savior has a *limitless supply* of healing power. Boldly come before His throne of grace and ask for healing. But when you ask, beware. You may hear the evil one whisper that you are not important enough; that Jesus is too busy; that you have already asked. Don't listen. These are lies!

You are important.

You are valuable.

You are worthy.

Jesus is never too busy for you—ever. Jesus has more than enough time and more than enough power to answer all of our prayers. Never stop praying for yourself and for others.

> *Jesus is never too busy for you—ever. Jesus has more than enough time and more than enough power to answer all of our prayers.*

I've seen God's healing power work on more than one occasion. For example, following is a story from my Aunt Peggy. I share her words with her permission. As you read them, I hope they strengthen your faith.

On August 2, 2002, at forty-eight years of age, I suffered a major stroke that paralyzed the right side of my body. As word spread that I had suffered a stroke, friends, family, and coworkers prayed.

After two weeks in the hospital, my doctors moved me to a stroke rehabilitation facility for intense speech, occupational, and physical therapy. Just fourteen days into therapy, I experienced severe chest pain. I couldn't breathe. The doctors found that remnants of a large blood clot filled my lungs. They couldn't believe I was even alive.

They were debating how to treat my blood clots, possibly by giving me large doses of blood thinner to stop clot formation. With the blood thinner came great risks, but without it I would most likely die. I had no good option. My sister and I prayed and decided I should accept the doctor's recommendation to take the large doses of blood thinner. Fear of the unknown moved in and took root in my heart, so I prayed, "Please protect me from another stroke, God."

Thankfully, I didn't suffer another stroke. But progress was slow. During this time, my niece, Wendy, came to visit. I shared with her all that had happened and explained that doctors concluded it would take at least six months to a year for the clots in my lungs to dissolve. Even then there would likely be permanent scarring. Wendy asked if she could pray a healing prayer over me. Of course I said yes!

She laid her hands on my chest, directly over my lungs. As she prayed, I felt warmth emanating from her hands. I knew "something" was happening. I had been weeping through her prayer. But at one point, my crying turned to sobbing as I sensed the very presence of God in that room and in my body. I will never, ever forget that moment.

Two weeks later, at my request, doctors took another scan of my lungs to determine the status of the clots over which Wendy prayed. They felt the scan was not only unnecessary but useless since it takes six months to a year for the clots to dissolve. I insisted, though, so they finally conceded and ordered the scan.

May I tell you the results of the scan? With the exception of a few small remnants, my lungs were free of any clots! Just three weeks before, my husband had described my right lung as looking like it was filled with shotgun pellets. And now there was nearly nothing to be seen on that scan!

The doctors were surprised and shocked, but, of course, attributed it to the blood thinner working much faster than they had expected or ever seen. But my husband and I knew the *real* truth: the power of healing prayer.

Isn't that amazing? Now, over a decade later, my aunt has regained 100 percent use of her arm and leg! She praises God daily that He spared her life, returned her speech, healed her lungs, and restored her limbs to full functioning order. She believes God healed and restored her to bring her out on the other side a stronger woman and Christian, able to testify to His faithfulness and bring glory and honor to His name.

What seemingly impossible mental or emotional health issue are you facing today? I encourage you now to reach out and touch the hem of Jesus' garment.

Do you believe God can heal you, both physically and emotionally? Ask Him to help you with your unbelief. He will be faithful!

Take time to review your lesson and prayerfully answer the questions below based on what you have learned from God's Word and what God has spoken into your heart throughout your time with Him.

Who is *Jehovah Rapha*?

What does this mean for my life?

Prayer:

Jehovah Rapha, thank You that You are my Healer. Heal me completely in my body, mind, heart, and soul. Take my open wounds and heal them by the power of Your blood. Enable me to see each one as a beautiful scar, representing Your faithfulness and Your healing work in my life. May I use each scar to testify to You and bring glory and honor to Your name.

Optional Video Study

Use the space below to note anything that stands out to you from the video teaching. You may also choose to take notes on a separate sheet of paper.

Use the following questions as a guide for group discussion:

What one thing stood out to you most in this chapter?

How can you apply the name of God you studied this week to your own life and current situation?

Take a few moments to review this week's memory verse together. What does this verse mean to you personally?

Could you relate to any of the people or situations from the Bible that you studied this week? If so, how?

CHAPTER FIVE

More Magnificent Names

Prayer:

Heavenly Father, Your Word says that those who know Your name will trust in You. Thank You for all You have taught me about Yourself as You have revealed Your names to me.

Today, I embark on learning more of Your attributes. Open my mind and teach me as I seek to know You more intimately. Lord, speak to my heart. Teach me to understand that which on my own I could never learn. Through the power of Your Holy Spirit, grant me wisdom and understanding beyond my years. I am an empty vessel. Pour into me, Lord, until I am overflowing! I ask this all in Jesus' name. Amen.

Part One: Jehovah Shalom: The One Who Brings Me Peace

Memory Verse: So Gideon built an altar to the LORD there and called it the LORD Is Peace.

—Judges 6:24 (NIV)

I pray that unveiling the names of God has not only deepened your understanding of God but also your relationship with Him. God's names reveal in a fresh way the eternal realities of who He is—His magnificence, His authority, His dominion, His sovereignty, and His purposes. Today we meet God through another of His great names, *Jehovah Shalom*—The Lord Is Peace.

Before we jump into our lesson, let's take another trip back in time to a story that centers on the Midianites, the descendants of Ishmael. (Remember he was Hagar's son.) The first time we learn of the land of Midian is when Moses fled there after Pharaoh tried to kill him (Exodus 2:15). While there, Moses married a Midianite woman named Zipporah.

Near the end of Moses' life, one of Israel's greatest enemies, the Moabites, aligned themselves with the Midianites. From that point on, the Midianites and the Israelites became bitter enemies. The Midianites continually attempted—and many times succeeded—in seducing God's people into pagan worship and sexual immorality. Eventually, God commanded Moses to destroy the Midianites (Numbers 25:16–17). The Israelites obeyed and attacked the Midianites, killing every man and destroying every town (Numbers 31). This created a deep-seated hatred of God's chosen people within the hearts of the surviving Midianites.

Two hundred years later, God's people again walked in disobedience. Because of their disobedience, God brought judgment upon His people, as He had done in the past. This time He delivered the Israelites into the hands of the Midianites for seven years (Judges 6).

Read Judges 6–7 for more on this history.

As had become their custom, God's people repented, and God, in His faithfulness, listened and answered. This time He raised up a man named Gideon—an ordinary young man from an ordinary family—to do an extraordinary thing. Gideon lived in the town of Ophrah, located near the border of Midian. An angel of the Lord appeared to him and called him to lead a battle against the Midianites: "The Eternal One is with you, mighty warrior ... Go out with your strength and rescue Israel from the oppression of Midian" (Judges 6:12, 14).

Read Judges 6:15. How did Gideon respond when God spoke to him?

Gideon's words reveal that he was living not by faith but by sight! The Midianites were stronger and more powerful than the Israelites. They were a cruel, evil people who took great pleasure and pride in terrorizing the Israelites every chance they got. Consequently, God's people greatly feared the Midianites. They felt God had abandoned them, and Gideon could not imagine God using him to defeat this menacing enemy. Yet pay attention to how God referred to Gideon.

Reread Judges 6:15. What did the angel of the Lord call Gideon?

God saw *who* Gideon would become as he stepped out in faith, and God called him by that name. Friend, if Gideon had not "changed" his mind; if he had not stepped out in faith, if he had not stepped into his new name, he never would have won this great victory, and he never would have been featured in the Hebrews' "Hall of Faith" (Hebrews 11:32).

Have you ever been in a situation similar to that which Gideon faced, unable to reconcile God's truths and promises in His Word with what you were personally walking through? What questions did you ask God?

Read 1 Corinthians 1:26–29. Write out these verses in your own words. Although Gideon did not have this promise, we do. How does this verse speak to you in your current circumstances?

God met Gideon in his place of fear and doubt and reassured him. He promised Gideon that He would be with him and that Gideon would be successful. Sadly, this was not enough for Gideon.

Read Judges 6:17. What did Gideon ask of God?

Gideon then offered God a sacrifice.

🖋 **Read Judges 6:20–21.** What did God do in response to Gideon's request?

🖋 What did Gideon realize in that moment? What was his emotion?

God lovingly responded to Gideon: "Don't be afraid, Gideon. Be at peace. You will not die" (Judges 6:23).

🖋 **Read Judges 6:24.** In response to God's words of assurance, what did Gideon do next?

🖋 Write down the name Gideon gave the altar.

The King James Version says, "Gideon called it … Jehovah Shalom." We will delve into this name of God in just a bit, but let's wrap up Gideon's story first.

🖋 According to Judges 6:25–27, what happened later that night?

Gideon's initial act called for great courage. And even though he did it in the dark of night with great fear and trepidation, he responded with one small step of obedience. That step was followed by another and another. In the end, Gideon not only won the battle, but he won it with only three hundred soldiers!

This is how God works. I have said it before and I will say it again. In story after story, blessings follow obedience. God is always present and working every step of the way.

This account gives me great encouragement, and I pray it does you as well.

Is there something to which God is calling you that you think you cannot do? What keeps you from saying yes to God? Do you lack confidence in your skills and abilities? Your finances? Your time? Your education?

When God calls us, He commissions us. When He commissions us, He equips us. Scripture says it best in Hebrews 13:21: God equips those He calls. He is faithful to finish every work He begins.

When God calls us, He commissions us. When He commissions us, He equips us.

Read Judges 6 again. As you reflect on your own life, is there something seemingly beyond your ability to which God is calling you? If there is, find the courage and the strength to say, "Yes, Lord, here I am. I am willing." Write a prayer of commitment, asking God to help you rely on His Word and His promises to accomplish what He has set before you.

In the midst of the call and the praying for direction, remember Gideon's story and how God revealed Himself to Gideon in His name *Jehovah Shalom*. The Lord is Peace promises to be with you!

Digging Deeper

Now let's better examine God's name *Jehovah Shalom*. *Jehovah* is the Jewish national name of God. God chose it as His personal name, the name by which He related to and interacted with His covenant people, the Israelites. *Shalom* as a noun means "peace, completeness." It means much more than a cessation of war or hostilities; it comes from the root verb *shalom*, which means to be whole, "complete, perfect, and full."[1]

Gideon knew God was promising well-being, health, and prosperity. With this promise, Gideon gained confidence; he knew God could not only use him but also win a victory with him.

Friend, whenever God calls us to a task that we think is beyond us, the key is to keep our eyes on God, not our circumstances. To keep our minds fixed on His character. To keep our hearts fixed on His promises.

Whenever God calls us to a task that we think is beyond us, the key is to keep our eyes on God, not our circumstances.

🖋 What did God ask Abraham in Genesis 18:14?

🖋 What does the angel of the Lord say to Mary in Luke 1:37?

🖋 What does Jeremiah pray to God in Jeremiah 32:17?

🖋 What does Jesus say to His disciples in Matthew 19:26?

🖋 What does Paul testify in Philippians 4:13?

How can we be filled with God's *shalom*? There is one way and one way only—Jesus.

🖋 **Read Isaiah 9:6.** What is one of Jesus' names in this verse?

Jesus is the Prince of Peace! He is our peace. When we invite Jesus into our lives, He comes to reside within us. And we not only get Jesus, but we get the fruit of the Holy Spirit. One of those fruits is peace (Galatians 5:22). Jesus is the *source* of our peace. In Him and Him alone do we find *shalom*—completeness, wholeness, well-being, confidence. Without Him, we will never experience that perfect peace.

How do we live in the fullness of God's peace? We find clear direction in Proverbs 3:1–17.

Read Proverbs 3:1–17. Write out verses 13 and 17.

List the many blessings of wisdom found in this passage.

The last verse states that "all" her ways are pleasant and "all" her paths are peace. This peace is not the temporary, conditional peace we find in this world. It's an eternal, everlasting peace that consumes us from the inside out. It's the peace that passes all understanding. Friend, when we walk in this peace, God promises it will guard our hearts and minds.

It's our choice whether we take hold of that peace and walk in the fullness of it. It's ours to have. But walking in the fullness of God's peace comes only as we study, learn, submit to, and live out (obey) God's Word.

Apply It

One of my favorite devotional books is *Keep a Quiet Heart* by Elisabeth Elliot, a godly author, speaker, and teacher of the Word. She says this about peace:

Prayerlessness is one of many ways by which we can easily forfeit the peace God wants us to have. I've been thinking of some other ways ...

1. Resent God's ways.

2. Worry as much as possible.

3. Pray only about things you can manage yourself.

4. Refuse to accept what God gives you.

5. Look for peace elsewhere than in Him.

6. Try to rule your own life.

7. Doubt God's word.

8. Carry all your cares.[2]

Do you struggle with one of these? I am struggling right now with number five. So many times I find my peace in completing my daily tasks. If everything is checked off my "to do" list, I end my day in great peace. But if there are some items left to carry to the next day, I grow anxious, wondering if I will find the time tomorrow to get both days' tasks done.

Mrs. Elliot follows her list above with eight ways *not* to forfeit our peace. She presents the truths below as antidotes for our worrisome ways.

1. "Great peace have those who love your law, and nothing can make them stumble" (Psalm 119:165 NIV).

2. "Do not be anxious about anything" (Philippians 4:6 NIV).

3. "But in every situation, by prayer and petition, with thanksgiving, present your requests to God" (Philippians 4:6–7 NIV).

4. "Take my yoke upon you and learn from me ... and you will find rest for your souls" (Matthew 11:29 NIV).

5. "Peace I leave with you; my peace I give you. I do not give to you as the world gives. Do not let your hearts be troubled and do not be afraid" (John 14:27 NIV).

6. "Let the peace of Christ rule in your hearts" (Colossians 3:15 NIV).

7. "May the God of hope fill you with all joy and peace as you trust in him, so that you may overflow with hope by the power of the Holy Spirit" (Romans 15:13 NIV).

8. "Cast all your anxiety on him because he cares for you" (1 Peter 5:7 NIV).[3]

How I treasure these verses, each one promising and directing me how to live in the fullness of God's peace.

Take a moment to review Mrs. Elliot's list of ways we often forfeit our peace, identify the one with which you struggle most, and place a check mark next to it. Now, review the list of "antidotes," truths from God's Word that can override that worry. Next to the item with which you most struggle, take that negative thought—that lie you've believed—captive by writing down the truth of God's Word. Then spend some time in prayer, asking for God's help to replace your unbelief with peace. Finally, take a moment to put your prayer on paper, asking for God's help in replacing your unbelief with peace.

Here's my prayer:

Heavenly Father, take my eyes off my "to do" list. Remind me how You will enable me to finish everything that You have called me to do. If what I'm doing is not of You, make it clear. And in the midst of this day and the next, give me Your peace—not the peace the world gives, not the peace that finds its comfort in accomplishing tasks—but Your peace, which guards my heart and mind. Let me not be troubled, worried, or afraid, for I trust in You and walk confidently wrapped in Your peace. I ask this in Jesus' name. Amen!

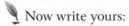 Now write yours:

Take time to review your lesson and prayerfully answer the questions below based on what you have learned from God's Word and what God has spoken into your heart throughout your time with Him.

Who is *Jehovah Shalom*?

What does this mean for my life?

Part Two:
All-Consuming Fire:
The One Who Is Jealous for You

Memory Verse: My name is Jealous, and I am a jealous God.

—Exodus 34:14

Jealousy. It's a word loaded with negative connotations. Why then does God call Himself a jealous God? Because, as is so often true, our human experience cannot comprehend God's divine ways. Isaiah 55:8–9 says it best: "My intentions are not always yours, and I do not go about things as you do. My thoughts and My ways are above and beyond you, just as heaven is far from your reach here on earth."

What images or memories does the word *jealousy* conjure up in your mind? For me, this word points to one of the lowest points in my marriage, a time that I don't often think about anymore, let alone like to share. My husband Monty and I began our marriage in a very difficult place. Eleven months before we walked down the aisle, I was raped by an armed masked man hiding in my apartment. Being a newlywed is difficult enough without bringing in such heavy baggage.

This horrific experience damaged me deeply from the inside out. And though I tried counseling and other medical methods of healing, it seemed as if healing would never come.

I lived most days donning a mask. Few knew that fear, anger, loneliness, and despair ruled my life. I tried to be a "good wife" and make my husband happy. But I just couldn't. Intimacy was too hard. It brought back too many terrible memories.

eft to play basketball or go to dinner with friends, I became frus-
trated and angry, pouting and crying, complaining that he needed
to put me first.

This caused an enormous rift in our marriage. Days were hard
and nights were long. Soon I began to imagine Monty looking elsewhere for the companionship he lacked with me. I needed to know
where he was at all times and who he was with. When I couldn't
get in touch with him, I would panic, my mind going to places and
imagining things it shouldn't. Jealousy consumed me. And believe
me, jealousy is an emotion that destroys everything in its path.

However, this destructive earthly jealousy is not the same as
God's jealousy. The crux of our lesson today is to gain an understanding of God's heavenly jealousy.

Scripture teaches that our Lord is a jealous God who loves
us wholly and completely, without condition, and who, in return,
demands our wholehearted love and full devotion. He is also an All-
Consuming Fire, who will ultimately destroy whatever is opposed
to His holiness.

> My name is Jealous, and I am a jealous God. (Exodus 34:14)

> Be careful not to forget the covenant of the LORD your God that he
> made with you; do not make for yourselves an idol in the form of
> anything the LORD your God has forbidden. For the LORD your God
> is a consuming fire, a jealous God. (Deuteronomy 4:23–24 NIV)

> So be very careful! Don't forget the covenant the Eternal your
> God made with you; don't make yourselves an idol in the shape of
> anything. The Eternal your God has commanded you not to! The
> Eternal your God burns with jealousy when you're not completely
> loyal to Him. (Deuteronomy 4:23–24)

210

The dictionary defines *jealousy* as "mental uneasiness from sus-picion or fear of rivalry, unfaithfulness." As jealousy grows, it's no longer just a feeling of uneasiness; it becomes a mental obsession that feeds you lies. My jealousy had become just that. How ashamed I am now of how I acted and treated this good and godly man with whom God had blessed me.

However, as God opened the door of my heart to His healing, the jealousy began to subside. Why? Because in Christ, I had finally found my "true first love." Until that time, I thought I had found that love in Monty. But I confused love and need. I saw Monty as my savior. He was my defender, my protector from the evil in the world. As long as I was with him, I would be safe. The thought of losing him terrified me because I truly did not think that I could live without him.

What I just described is a very unhealthy relationship. We should never "need" our husbands, our children, or anyone else, in this way. Ironically, I was so afraid of losing Monty that I treated him in a way that could potentially have driven him away.

No one on this earth can ever be our savior. We have only one Savior, and His name is Jesus.

No one on this earth can ever be our savior. We have only one Savior, and His name is Jesus.

In time, my healing came as I opened God's Word. I met God and His Son, Jesus, in a new way, and I began a new love relation-ship with God. As I did, He put my marriage in perspective. God became my first love. Monty became the gift God had given me on this earth to reveal His love to me. As God took His rightful place on the throne of my heart, Monty took his rightful place as well. Our marriage changed dramatically as I no longer lived consumed by jealousy.

In marriage, jealousy does have a place. Both husband and wife ought to feel a strong love and devotion for one another that they feel for no other person. Because of that fierce love, they should remain faithful to one another in every way. This is zealous love—healthy jealousy.

But when that jealousy goes awry, as it did in me, it can burn and scorch a marriage in the most destructive ways. We must work to prevent rival affections from arising in our hearts, and we must work to prevent lying and deceptive imaginations from arising in our minds. Both are threats to a happy and blessed marriage.

Of course, I never want to lose Monty, but I have come to know that I could and would be able to live without him. He and my children are the greatest gifts God has given me, and I love them with all my heart. But I hold them loosely because they are God's first, and then mine.

My hope is that by defining and discussing earthly jealousy, we'll have a truer understanding of God's jealousy. His jealousy is never an unhealthy or destructive thing. In fact, it is not a "thing" at all. God's jealousy is an attribute of God, so near to Him that it is one of His names.

God's jealousy is never an unhealthy or destructive thing. In fact, it is not a "thing" at all. God's jealousy is an attribute of God, so near to Him that it is one of His names.

Digging Deeper

Moses first introduces us to this name of God, *Jealous*, in Exodus 34:14. Nowhere else in Scripture do we see God's jealousy more clearly on display than in this part of Moses' life.

Before we dig into this Scripture, let's gain a bit of perspective as to where we are on Moses' journey. In Exodus 20, God gave Moses the Ten Commandments on the top of Mount Sinai.

Read Exodus 20. Which commands speak of God as being a jealous God?

Moses came down from the mountain and shared with the Israelites what God had spoken to him. God then called Moses back up the mountain to offer a sacrifice, to confirm the covenant He had made, and to receive the Ten Commandments on stone tablets. Here is the author's description (most believe the author to be Moses himself) of that time on the mountain:

> Moses made his way up the mountain. A *thick* cloud blanketed the mountain because the Eternal's glory had settled upon it … For the Israelites below, the Eternal's glory appeared to be a

consuming fire on the top of the mountain. As Moses walked further toward the top, he was swallowed by the cloud *of God's glory*, and he remained there for *a total of* 40 days and 40 nights. (Exodus 24:15–18)

What an incredible image! We find another of God's names here: *Consuming Fire*. I chose The Voice translation because of its choice of words: Moses "was swallowed by the cloud *of God's glory*." Oh, that we would know the sensation of being swallowed up in the glory of our God!

When God had finished giving Moses His instructions, He gave Moses two stone tablets inscribed by His own hand (Exodus 31:18; 32:15–16)! These tablets contained the Ten Commandments. Sadly, as Moses descended from this intimate time with God, he met with complete chaos at the bottom of the mountain.

Read Exodus 32:1–4, 19–20. What did Moses find, and what did he do in response?

Read Exodus 32:30–35.

Moses, although angry and disgusted, immediately interceded on behalf of the Israelites. He begged God to forgive His people. Moses served as their mediator, just as Christ is ours. God made clear that He would surely punish all who sinned, but then assured Moses that He would not revoke His covenant nor His promise to take the people into the land.

Time and time again God warned Israel not to participate in the practices of the pagan nations around them. He repeatedly issued commands for them to destroy pagan altars, idols, and high places. And each time they disobeyed. God grew weary.

I often wonder if God does the same with us. *Tolerance* is such a popular word today. We live in a pluralistic society composed of many different cultural, ethnic, and religious backgrounds. Political bodies are redefining marriage, family, and sexual identity. Yes, as Christians we should tolerate and respect others, treating each other kindly so that we can live peaceably. But this same tolerance can be a very dangerous, slippery slope, especially when it comes to matters of faith and Christianity.

The Bible makes it abundantly clear that we are not to "mix" our faith with the faiths of others. That is what God taught Noah, Abraham, Isaac, Jacob, Moses, and the prophets, and it is what Jesus taught. It may sound good to take a dash of Hinduism, a sprinkle of the New Age movement, and a bit of Buddhism and mix those together with Christianity to get a "good tasting" result, but such faith is not pure. It is not the faith to which God has called His people.

God is a Jealous God who demands loyalty and obedience. He's not interested in making our lives happy, my friend. He's interested solely in making us holy—more like Him. We are created in His image. He will not compete with other gods, with other religions, with other movements. One day they will all burn in His *All-Consuming Fire*. All that will remain is worship of the one true God! He will share His glory with no one and nothing.

Let me say that again: God will share His glory with no one and nothing.

God is not interested in making our lives happy, my friend. He's interested solely in making us holy, more like Him.

We see God deal directly with this issue of competition and tolerance as we arrive at a turning point in Exodus 33–34. God told Moses to tell the people to continue on to the land He had promised, but that He would not go with them because of their unfaithfulness. Moses, desperate once again for God's favor, went alone into the presence of the Lord and pleaded with Him to remain with them (Exodus 33:12–17). Because of His great love for Moses, God agreed, speaking these words: "You have gained my trust and blessing, and I know you by name" (Exodus 34:17).

God then told Moses to chisel out two stone tablets like the first ones and to meet with Him again on the mountain. Moses obeyed. Upon his arrival, the Lord came down in a cloud and stood there with Moses and made a powerful proclamation.

Read Exodus 34:5–7. What does God declare about Himself?

What are your favorite parts of this proclamation of who God is? Why?

This is an absolutely glorious definition of God's character. And if you read throughout the Old Testament, you will see it repeated again and again! (See Psalm 86:15; 103:6–8; Jonah 4:2.)

Read Exodus 34:7. What do you think the last sentence of that verse means?

When God speaks of "punishing" the children and their children for the sin of the fathers for the generations to come, most theologians understand this to mean not that the later generations will have to carry the *guilt* for the sins of the father, but rather that they will suffer the *consequences* of the sins of the father.

God will not remove the consequences of our sin. Said another way, children and grandchildren will not be condemned for the sins of their ancestors, but they will most likely suffer because of those sins.

Do you see examples of this truth in your own family history?

What can we do today to prevent the revisiting of this "curse" on our families?

God then makes another covenant with Moses in Exodus 34:10–28.

Read Exodus 34:10–14. As God renews His covenant with the Israelites, He promises to perform wonders so that others will see how much He loves and favors His chosen people (verse 10). But God also requires something of His people as a condition of His covenant promises. List the first three conditions in verses 11–13.

Write out verse 14 below.

God declared His name: "Jealous." This comes from the Hebrew word *qanah* and means "to be jealous or to be zealous." When God is the subject of the verb *qanah*, the meaning is "be zealous." Unlike human jealousy, which is motivated by human self-centeredness, God's jealousy is holy and pure. God will not tolerate rivalry and unfaithfulness. He demands wholehearted devotion. Deuteronomy 4:24 says, "For the LORD your God is a consuming fire, a jealous God" (NIV). He knew that if the hearts of His people wandered, they would fall into sin. And this proved itself true over and over again as the Israelites allied themselves with, did business with, worshiped with, and intermarried with the pagan nations around them. Every time they walked in disobedience to God's command to love and worship Him alone, it dragged them deeper and deeper into sin and rebellion.

God is not some big ogre in the sky, just waiting to dominate and punish us. No, He is jealous for our affections because He loves us with a most amazing, unconditional, everlasting love. God wants our undivided love and attention. He desires a deep and personal intimate relationship with us. He knows that only when we set our hearts on Him and Him alone will we receive the abundant life He promises.

God is not some big ogre in the sky, just waiting to dominate and punish us. No, He is jealous for our affections because He loves us with a most amazing, unconditional, everlasting love.

What is so marvelous about God's love is that what we could not achieve on our own, He stepped in and did for us. Our Jealous God intervened in the most selfless way possible. He sent His one and only Son to die on the cross to redeem His stubborn, obstinate, unfaithful, disobedient people. The cross at Calvary put His Jealous Love on display for all to see!

Read Romans 5:6–11. How does Paul describe those for whom Christ died?

God did this for us when we were yet sinners. For those of us who are saved children of God—who have given our lives to Him—how much more does His jealous love mean to us now? To you personally?

Don't miss this, my friend. God didn't wait for us to be "better," more well-behaved children before He sent Jesus to die for us. He did it while we were weak, while we were still shrouded in sin, while we were His enemies. He did it *in spite of* who we were.

And, now, because of His great love, we have been made righteous in His eyes through the blood of His Son. Reconciled. Made right. There is now *no* condemnation for those who are in Christ Jesus (Romans 8:1). God's grace is enough. No matter what keeps you from coming to God—no matter the idols, no matter the sin, no matter the unfaithfulness—He forgives. His love is enough!

> *God didn't wait for us to be "better," more well-behaved children before He sent Jesus to die for us.*

Apply It

I encourage you to remember each day that nothing can ever separate you from the love of God (Romans 8:38–39). Circumstances will come into our lives that will make us feel like He has forgotten us. We will disobey and rebel in ways that will make us feel unworthy to receive God's love ever again. In these times, we must remember to pray and address our heart's cry to the Jealous One, the God who loves us with an everlasting love—the God who will never leave us or forsake us.

Read Romans 8:31–35. Take time to prayerfully write each verse in your own words, personalizing it for your circumstances.

My cherished friend, once you are God's child, your name is engraved on the palm of His hand. And He will never, ever let you go! He has a jealous, passionate everlasting love for you that nothing and no one can ever take away.

Are there things in your life that take a higher position than God? Your children, your husband, ministry, health, fears, anxieties, past mistakes, addictions, entertainment, material things? Do you desire any of these more than you desire God, *or* do you fear any of these things more than you trust God?

Reflect on your own life and honestly evaluate who or what is most important to you. Write a prayer surrendering those things, feelings, people or emotions. As you write this prayer, remember that the One to whom you are surrendering has a jealous love for you and will move mountains to be your number one priority!

Take time to review your lesson and prayerfully answer the questions below based on what you have learned from God's Word and what God has spoken into your heart throughout your time with Him.

Who is our *Jealous God, the All-Consuming Fire*?

What does this mean for my life?

Part Three:
El Elyon:
The One Who Is Exalted Above All Others

Memory Verse: For you, LORD, are the Most High over all the earth; you are exalted far above all gods.

—Psalm 97:9 (NIV)

I can find no better story in all of Scripture than the following to illustrate what it means to worship God as *El Elyon,* the God Most High. Travel back with me in the gospel of John to a very special dinner party.

We encounter Mary (sister of Martha and Lazarus) at a dinner given in Jesus' honor. All the guests have arrived and the delicious aromas of roasted meat and freshly baked bread fill the room. In the silence of the heavens, the angels, the saints, and God Himself are preparing for the evil and injustice that is about to come to Jesus, the Son of God.

Jesus, in fact, had told many of those at the dinner that "the Son of Man will be handed over to be crucified" (Matthew 26:2 NIV). But of all the people present, I believe only one woman really understood Jesus' words. Mary had been sitting at Jesus' feet for three years, listening to His every Word. She sensed in her heart what was about to happen to her Lord and Savior, so she felt compelled to express her love and gratitude to Him. Gratitude for all that Jesus had done for their family, most especially for raising her brother, Lazarus, from the dead. And love for what He was about to do for all mankind.

She wanted to give Jesus a gift, something special, something extravagant. She held in her hands an alabaster jar of expensive perfumed oil. The estimated value of the jar and its contents was nearly a year's wages. Without a doubt, it was her most precious and valuable possession.

She slipped quietly to Jesus' side and knelt at His feet. I can only imagine the gentle way in which Jesus looked upon her and the tender smile she received as she looked up into His eyes. Without any hesitation, Mary broke the seal and extravagantly poured the fragrant oil on Jesus' feet. And as the contents flowed out, her tears flowed as well, tears representing her overwhelming love for Jesus and her sorrow for what was about to befall Him.

In this simple, yet profound and selfless act of loving devotion, Mary revealed her sold-out heart for God and for Jesus. Mary's was a beautiful act of worship to *El Elyon*, the God Most High. Her actions spoke more than a thousand words ever could. By breaking and pouring out the precious contents of her alabaster jar, she held nothing back. She gave it all! She knew she was giving everything she had to the One who was about to give her His all. She withheld nothing—not a single drop. And she expected nothing in return.

> *Mary revealed her sold-out heart for God and for Jesus ... She withheld nothing—not a single drop. And she expected nothing in return.*

Scripture says that in that moment, "the pleasant fragrance of this extravagant ointment filled the entire house" (John 12:3). The gift of her sacrificial love filled that room and it still fills our hearts today.

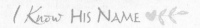

In response to Mary's selfless gift, Jesus honored her with these words: "I tell you this: the good news *of the kingdom of God* will be spread all over the world, *and wherever the good news travels,* people will tell the story of this woman and her good discipleship. And people will remember her" (Matthew 26:13).

Imagine Mary's emotions as Jesus' words washed over her heart! No matter what anyone else ever said, her Savior—her Lord—was pleased. He valued her precious, sacrificial gift.

Do you have an alabaster jar? A most treasured possession? Your children? Your marriage? A desire for a child or a husband? A longing? A dream? A career? Your bank account? Your health? Your time? Your reputation? The right to be right? Before we continue with our lesson today, prayerfully consider whether or not you are willing to pour it out at Jesus' feet—to surrender it to *El Elyon*, the God Most High.

Digging Deeper

The first person to call upon God as "the God Most High" was a mysterious, ancient king and priest. We meet him in a fascinating encounter with the patriarch Abram in Genesis 14:18–24. (Remember, this was Abraham's name before God changed it.) The author of Genesis identifies this mysterious man as a "priest of the One whom He called 'the God Most High'" (Genesis 14:18b).

Read Genesis 14:18–20.

Upon Abram's victorious return from battle, he encountered two men: the king of Sodom and the king of Salem, also identified as Melchizedek. Melchizedek presented Abram with bread and wine and blessed him in the name of "the God Most High, Creator of the Heavens and earth" or *El Elyon* (Genesis 14:19b).

El means "God." It denotes strength, might, and power. In our study, we have seen it combined with other words to identify different attributes of God. *El Roi. Elohim.* Now, combined with *Elyon*, it means "the God Most High" and stresses God's strength, sovereignty, and supremacy.

One interesting aspect of this story is that Melchizedek was most likely not a Jew. His heritage is unknown to this day. It's as if he appeared for this moment in time and then disappeared, never to be seen again. Why is this significant? Because it reveals that the Jews were not the only people who recognized Yahweh (Jehovah) as the one true God. Melchizedek, by using this name of God, recognized God's sovereign dominion over the earth and all its creatures.

Read Genesis 14:21–24. Who else recognized God as "the God Most High"?

We see Abram treat the king of Sodom with disdain, but he treats the king of Salem (Melchizedek) with great respect. Why do you think this is the case?

What differentiated the kings to Abram was that Melchizedek called his God by a name Abram recognized. In doing so, Abram recognized that their "Gods" were the same God. In other words, Melchizedek and Abram called God by different names, but they worshiped the same God.[4] Both acknowledged there was only one true God, the God Most High, the Creator of the heavens and earth.

Centuries later, we meet another non-Jew who recognized Israel's God as the God Most High.

🖋 **Read Daniel 4:1–34.** How does King Nebuchadnezzar come to worship and honor the God Most High?

Some believe the length of time between when King Nebuchadnezzar lost his sanity and when God restored it was seven years. What a long time to live in such confusion and despair!

🖋 What specific praises does King Nebuchadnezzar lift to God in Daniel 4:34–35?

🖋 **Read Daniel 4:36–37.** What happened to King Nebuchadnezzar once he surrendered to God and worshiped Him?

Early in his reign, King Nebuchadnezzar believed it was his own power and wisdom that led to the growth and success of his kingdom. Yet Daniel, through his interpretation of the king's dream, warned him: "You will be driven away from people and will live with the wild animals; you will eat grass like the ox. Seven times will pass by for you until you acknowledge that the Most High is sovereign over all kingdoms on earth and gives them to anyone he wishes" (Daniel 4:32 NIV). King Nebuchadnezzar learned, through these very tragic and humbling circumstances, that God is sovereign. It is He who rules according to His will. God uses kings and kingdoms, like Nebuchadnezzar, as mere instruments to accomplish His purposes.

Once Nebuchadnezzar humbled himself and acknowledged God as the God Most High, he rose to greater heights of honor than he had ever known!

Reread King Nebuchadnezzar's words of praise in Daniel 4:34–35. Now write your own words of praise to *El Elyon*.

This is further evidence of God's promise that blessings follow obedience, and that God exalts those who humble themselves. Abundant blessings and promises flow to the woman who trusts in God Most High. When emotional demands overwhelm us, unrelenting insecurities consume us, defeating thoughts overtake us, and anxieties entangle us, *El Elyon* is more than enough! The author of Psalm 91 pours out a powerful testimony to the refuge and strength found in our God Most High.

When emotional demands overwhelm us, unrelenting insecurities consume us, defeating thoughts overtake us, and anxieties entangle us, El Elyon is more than enough!

🖊 **Read Psalm 91.** The opening words are some of the most well-known in Scripture. Write down the names for God used in verses 1–2.

Believed to have been written by a priest or Levite, Psalm 91 offers great comfort for those who are fearful and troubled. In the very first verse, the author gives us the image of God as our protector—a God to whom we can run and find shelter from the storms of life. He is not a distant God. He is not an impersonal God. He is a loving God who calls us to Himself in times of trouble and distress.

There is no mountain of problems so high that God Most High is not higher still. Both this psalm and Psalm 17 speak of God covering us with His feathers, hiding us in the shadow of His wings. Like a mama bird protects her babies, God protects us. In fact, in the last few verses of Psalm 16, the author lists *El Elyon*'s promises to those who truly love and trust Him.

> *There is no problem so high that God Most High is not higher still.*

🖊 **Read Psalm 91:14–16.**

🖊 Write these verses in the form of a proclamation—promises you can hold close to your heart to encourage you and carry you through difficult times. Here's my prayer of proclamation as an example:

Thank You, El Elyon, that You are my refuge and my fortress. Because You love me, I am Yours. I belong to You, and You will rescue me. You will cover me with Your feathers and hide me under Your wings. Because I acknowledge Your name, You will protect me. When I call upon You, You will answer me. You will be with me in trouble. You will deliver me and honor me. With long life You will satisfy me and show me Your salvation. Thank You, El Elyon, that no matter the height of my mountain, You are higher still. In You I find my hope and my rest. I pray this in Jesus' name. Amen.

Now I invite you to craft your own prayer. Feel free to base it on any or all of the verses in Psalm 91.

Apply It

Let's take a look now at how we can connect *El Elyon* with Jesus—the radiance of God's glory. Just as you cannot separate the sun from its brilliance, you cannot separate the Son's radiance from the glory of His Father.

Just as you cannot separate the sun from its brilliance, you cannot separate the Son's radiance from the glory of His Father.

God and Jesus are one. Jesus is not merely a reflection of God; He is God. Take a look at these verses.

- In Luke 1:32, Luke identified Jesus as the "Son of the Highest God."

- In Mark 5:7, a demon called out to Jesus in fear: "Jesus, Son of the Most High."

- In Matthew 3:17, God Himself identified Jesus: "This is my Son, whom I love; this is the Apple of my eye; with him I am well pleased."

Read Hebrews 1:3–4.

When you face what seems to be an insurmountable mountain to climb, remember these truths:

- Jesus now sits at the right hand of His Father in heaven and intercedes with the Father on *your* behalf (Romans 8:34).

- Nothing can separate *you* from the love of God that is in Christ Jesus (Romans 8:38).

- In *all* things *you* are more than a conqueror through Jesus who loved you enough to die for *you* (Romans 8:37).

- And finally, when you do have to walk through the fiery trial, God makes a promise to *you* in Romans 8:28.

What is that promise in Romans 8:28?

In all things, the good and the bad, *El Elyon* works for your good. He uses your circumstances to conform you to the likeness of His Son—to make you more like Him.

You can trust that the God Most High has *you* in His care!

Pray to *El Elyon*, letting the Holy Spirit lead you. Use the following steps to guide you, and write down your prayer if you like.

1. Praise God as *El Elyon* (because He is the God above all gods, the Name above all names).

2. Confess to *El Elyon* (anything interfering with your ability to trust Him as the God Most High).

3. Thank *El Elyon* (for all He has revealed in this new name of God).

4. Invite *El Elyon* (to help set your heart on heavenly, rather than earthly, things).

Take time to review your lesson and prayerfully answer the questions below based on what you have learned from God's Word and what God has spoken into your heart throughout your time with Him.

Who is *El Elyon*?

What does this mean for my life?

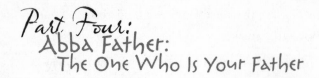

Part Four:
Abba Father:
The One Who Is Your Father

> **Memory Verse:** The Spirit you have received adopts you *and welcomes you* into God's own family. That's why we call out to Him, "Abba! Father!" *as we would address a loving daddy. Through that prayer,* God's Spirit confirms in our spirits that we are His children.
>
> —Romans 8:15b–16

For twenty-nine years the world knew my husband by one name, Monty. Oh, he had some nicknames that he may not appreciate me sharing, but to most everyone in the world, he was Monty. However, when he turned twenty-nine years old, he received another name—a very precious and personal name—Daddy. Well, it may have started as "Da Da," but it was a new name that changed Monty's life forever. We now have two children, Lauren and Bo, who call him by that name. His new name carried, and continues to carry, with it great blessings and great responsibilities. And for the record, he is an amazing father.

God has also given Monty a heart for young men. For the last several years, he has coached an AAU basketball team and served as an assistant coach for the varsity men's basketball team at our son's high school. Because some of these young men don't know their fathers at all or have "absentee" fathers, they have come to feel like sons to Monty. He picks them up and takes them home from practice. He takes them to lunch and hangs out with them between games and after practice. He has even had to take a few boys to doctor appointments, games, or weekend tournaments because there is no one at home who can. Monty speaks into the lives of these young men on basketball, school attendance and grades, character development, and even spiritual development when God opens the door. These boys are *like* sons to him.

But Bo isn't *like* a son to Monty. Bo *is* his son.

Is there a distinction? Absolutely. Fatherhood is so much more than speaking into a child's life and investing time when it fits into your schedule. It's a God-given physical and spiritual bond that never ends, and nothing can ever take it away.

Scripture teaches that in addition to our earthly fathers, you and I have another Father. He is not *like* a Father. He *is* our Father. A Father with whom we will always have a bond—a bond that will never end and that can never be taken away.

Digging Deeper

We've spent quite a bit of time in the Old Testament during this study. But, in this lesson, let's look at the New Testament. This is where we meet God as our Abba Father, in Romans 8.

As a bit of background, in Romans 8:1–11, Paul taught that in God's eyes there are only two kinds of people—those who live by the flesh and those who live by the Spirit. Said another way, there are those who have been born once (physically) and those who have been born twice (physically and spiritually). When we enter this world as a baby, we live solely by our flesh. We seek to satisfy our natural, human desires. What does that mean? It means our minds are set on the things of this earth—on things that will gratify our physical needs and desires.

When we invite Jesus to be Lord and Savior of our lives, we are born again. We receive a new nature. God infuses us with new life through His Holy Spirit. Through that infusion, God empowers us to live differently. We begin to grow in our new nature and set our minds not on earthly things but on heavenly things.

Oh, don't get me wrong. We'll still battle our old nature, our flesh, because we live in a physical body and that body lures us into satisfying itself. But we are no longer fighting the battle alone because that infusion of God's Holy Spirit equips and empowers us. Isn't it good to know that God doesn't just give us the gift of His Spirit and then abandon us, leaving us on our own! He provides a way for us to live victoriously by the Spirit each and every day.

Read Romans 8:12–17.

Paul wrote in Romans 8:12 (NIV) that our new life "obligates" us to live according to our new nature, according to the Spirit. Make no mistake—we are totally incapable of doing this on our own. Yet God makes a way by altering His relationship with us.

Who does Paul say are those led by the Spirit (verse 14)?

What do we receive according to verse 15?

Paul used the analogy of slavery to help us understand his teaching. Among the Greeks and Romans, the law permitted a man who had no son to adopt one, even one not related to him. The law even allowed for him to adopt one of his slaves as a son. The adopted son not only took the name of the father but also was in every respect regarded and treated as a son. Indeed, he was as much the man's son as any of his natural-born children. He had the privilege of calling his former master by the title of "father." See Galatians 4:5–6.[5]

🖋 **Read Galatians 4:1–7.** How does this verse speak to the principles Paul taught in Romans 8:14–15?

Romans 8:15 teaches us that salvation releases us from the spirit of fear through the power of the Holy Spirit. What is meant by the spirit of fear? It means we are no longer slaves to the law, subject to follow the law out of fear of what will happen if we don't. We are no longer subject to the fear of death and to Satan, the one who holds the power of death over us.

> *We are no longer subject to the fear of death and to Satan, the one who holds the power of death over us.*

🖋 **Read 2 Timothy 1:7 and 1 John 4:18.** What do these verses say about fear?

Paul taught in Romans 8:15 that in place of the spirit of fear, we receive the spirit of sonship, meaning we are adopted into God's family. *Sonship* translates from the Greek word *huiothesia*, which combines two Greek words: *huios*, "a son," and *thesis*, "a placing."[6] It signifies the place and condition given to one to whom it does not naturally belong. In biblical times, it was a legal procedure whereby a person was taken from one family (or no family) and placed into a new family.

As applied to you and me, we have been taken from the family of Adam and placed into the family of God.[7] Jesus, by His very nature is God's Son, while we are made sons (and daughters) through adoption.

Let's revisit my story about Bo and the basketball boys: Bo, by his genetic makeup, is Monty's natural-born son; the boys on the basketball team are *like* sons to Monty. However, if Monty chose to adopt any of those boys, through an official, legal adoption process, they no longer would be *like* sons; they would be sons and become full-fledged members of our family. They would hold equal status with Bo in every way regarding rights and inheritance. That is the very same status we hold with God when we are adopted into His family.

And so let's take a look at what the Bible says about our Father. At the end of Romans 8:15, we find our next name of God.

In Romans 8:15, what do we cry?

The word *Abba* was the Aramaic word for "father." The word *father* is a translation of the Greek word *pater*.[8] Abba was the way young Jewish children addressed their fathers during Jesus' time. Modern equivalents are Daddy or Papa. Abba conveyed familiarity and closeness.

The Jews would never have dreamed of using such a personal term for God. Because they did not have an intimate relationship with God, they became bewildered when Jesus encouraged them to do just that.

We call God "Father" today because Jesus modeled that for us.

Read Mark 14:36. Write the words Jesus prayed.

Describe the state of Jesus' heart as He cried out to His Father in this prayer.

When Jesus prayed, almost without exception He addressed God with the name "Father." This verse reveals the rare occasion He used both Abba and Father, revealing the intensity of emotions churning within His spirit.

Let's return to Romans 8 for a moment and examine the rewards of the spirit of sonship.

Read Romans 8:17. List the three rewards or blessings of sonship.

First, we receive a new position in the eyes of God.

What does it mean to you to be a child of God? What are the benefits?

Second, we are heirs.

What does it mean to be an heir?

In our modern usage of that word, an heir is one who is due, but has not yet received, an inheritance. Biblically, it means we have actual possession of a future inheritance. We possess in Christ all God has for us. However, we don't get to enjoy the fullness of that inheritance now. It grows and matures with each day until we receive it in all its fullness the day we walk into eternity.

Third, we are coheirs (joint-heirs) with Christ.

I found this to be a little harder to comprehend, but I think Dr. David Jeremiah explained it well in his commentary on Romans:

> If a man dies, leaving a large farm to four heirs, the estate is divided evenly and each heir receives twenty-five percent of the whole. But if a man leaves a farm to four of his sons as joint-heirs, then each son owns the whole farm. Each one can say, "This house is mine; those barns are mine; those fields are mine." ... Thus when the Lord tells us that we are heirs of God and joint-heirs of Jesus Christ, we are being informed that everything that God the Father has given to the Lord Jesus Christ has been given us also.[9]

We don't get just one small fraction, our assigned part, of what God promised. Each and every believer receives a full portion of God and all His promises. Our heavenly Father has bequeathed to us an invaluable inheritance. No person could ever give us what the Father has promised because our God is the ultimate Gift-giver. He is the Author, Creator, and Sustainer of this world and the world to come; the Owner of all that is, was, or ever will be. And even more profoundly, God is not only the source of our inheritance, sweet friend. He *is* our inheritance.

Let me say it again: God is not only the source of our inheritance. He *is* our inheritance.

God is not only the source of our inheritance. He is our inheritance.

As I mentioned earlier, not only did Jesus call God His Father, but He taught us to call God *our* Father.

Read Matthew 6:9. Write down the opening words of Jesus' prayer.

It may seem redundant to keep stressing the Father-Son relationship between God and Jesus, but the frequency with which Jesus spoke of this relationship highlights its importance.

Read John 14:6–14. How many times does Jesus call God His Father?

What does Jesus say in verses 6 and 7 about how we get to the Father and get to know the Father?

What do verses 8–10 teach us about the relationship between Jesus and His Father?

Finally, what does Jesus say are the benefits we receive when we believe in the Father-Son relationship of which He speaks? (See verses 12–14.)

Apply It

As I have spent time studying the concept of God as our Abba Father, it truly blows my mind to think that the God of the universe not only allows me, but desires that I call Him by this intimate name. In the Old Testament, only a chosen few got to experience a personal and intimate relationship with God. In Christ, those who walked with Him received a better revelation of God. They saw Him incarnate, in the flesh. They walked, talked, and lived with Him for three years!

You and I receive an even greater gift; in fact, the greatest gift of all. When we receive Jesus as our Lord and Savior, our Abba Father implants Himself in our hearts. He lives within us. The Spirit of the Living God chooses to live inside you and me! Could there be any greater news?

The Spirit of the Living God chooses to live inside you and me! Could there be any greater news?

It's so easy to misunderstand your heavenly Father if you have or had a cruel, harsh, or absentee earthly father. It might even seem nearly impossible to understand God as a loving, caring Father because you never knew one. We tend to define God by what we know.

If you have or had a difficult relationship with your earthly father, will you open up the wounds in your heart and share them? Write a letter to God and release the emotions that hold your heart hostage and prevent you from fully understanding and trusting God as your Abba Father. Let me pray for you.

Heavenly Father, I know You know the hurt and anger filling this woman's heart. I thank You that You have rescued her from darkness and brought her into Your light. May she daily walk in the confidence of knowing that no matter who her earthly father is or was, You are now her Father. She is Your child, a child of the light.

Father, excise the hurt, shame, bitterness, anger, resentment, even hatred she may harbor in her heart. Expose every bit of it so that nothing, not a single particle, remains. Take her every thought captive to the obedience of Your Word. Help her, through the power of Your Holy Spirit, to acknowledge every hurtful incident, every abusive word or action. Lead her to confess any sin she harbors in her heart with regard to her father. Ensure that she knows You have fully forgiven her for those feelings. Remove any stain of sin with which the words and actions of her father have marked her. Enable her to see that in You she is made white as snow. Bathe her in Your love. Wash her with Your mercy and grace.

Thank You that the past is gone and any hold it once had on her is now broken by the blood of Jesus. Continue to keep Your hand upon her. Show her continually how much You love and care for her. Place the armor of God on her so she can stand against the memories and the strategies of the devil who would seek to take her back to the places of unforgiveness and anger. We thank You in advance that You will now go before her and be her rear guard and protect her heart and mind. We ask this in Jesus' name. Amen.

Take time to review your lesson and prayerfully answer the questions below based on what you have learned from God's Word and what God has spoken into your heart throughout your time with Him.

Who is my *Abba Father*?

What does this mean for my life?

Part Five: Study Wrap-Up

> **Memory Verse:** These are the words of the Amen, the Faithful and True Witness, the Beginning of God's creation.
>
> —Revelation 3:14

I have so enjoyed walking with you through the names and attributes of God and how Jesus fulfills those names. And now, because of what God has revealed to us as we've studied His Word, we can begin to call upon His names more and gain a deeper, richer relationship with our Heavenly Father. Whatever our trial, whatever our season of life, whatever our circumstances, we will find all we need in His names.

God is a promise-keeper. And Jesus, our Savior and Redeemer, is the guarantor of all those promises. Knowing the heart of God more intimately and being familiar with His attributes allows us to trust Him. Sometimes we doubt God's goodness. We distrust His intent. We question: *Does God really love me? Because if He did, He wouldn't have let this happen.* When these questions burden our hearts, I pray we can rest in what we now know because God has revealed it through the pages of His eternal, everlasting, never-changing Word.

God is faithful. He's the same yesterday, today, and forever. He has been faithful in the past. He will be faithful in the future. So we can trust He will also be faithful today.

God loves us. He sent Jesus to be the final, total, and complete expression of love for us.

God is so very near to us. He always has His eye upon us, watching over us, hiding us under the shadow of His wing. He will never leave us or forsake us.

God's Word stands for all eternity. He sent His living and active Word to speak into our every circumstance. Nothing trumps it. And not a single promise will ever fall from its pages.

No matter what, my friend, we can trust Him!

In his much loved Bible study, *Experiencing God,* Henry Blackaby reminds us just how much we can trust God.

Henry Blackaby and his wife heard the words no parent ever wants to hear: Your daughter has cancer. At sixteen, their daughter, Carrie, endured months of radiation and chemotherapy. They suffered along with their precious girl as they watched the toxic chemicals wreak havoc in her body. Some in their circle of friends blamed God, questioning whether He loved them anymore. But Blackaby and his wife didn't travel down that path. They didn't believe the serpent's hissing lie that God's love and character had changed.

How could they face this situation with such hope and assurance? Because long before this trial, Mr. and Mrs. Blackaby made a determination that no matter what their circumstances, they would always frame them against the backdrop of the cross. They believed in what the cross represents—the death of Jesus and His resurrection; God's final, total, and complete expression of love for His people. So when the "whys" and "what should we dos" arose, they still trusted. Upon seeing that cross, Blackaby resolved in his heart to trust God and prayed these words: *"Father,* don't ever let me look at circumstances and question Your love for me. Your love was settled on the cross. That has never changed and will never change for me." [10]

Carrie survived her cancer, and through that battle Mr. Blackaby said his faith never wavered because in the midst God assured Him, "All that I've ever accomplished for you is for such a time as this. This doesn't take you out of My will—this will show you what My will is. If your faith is not tested, you'll never know the dimensions of what I've provided."[11]

Oh friend, that we could all find that deep place of trust. That we would believe no matter what that God truly, deeply, and unwaveringly loves us.

If we believe in the magnificent names of God, if we trust in the unchanging character of God, if we trust in Jesus, we must let go of fear and doubt and dare to trust. No matter what our circumstances are, our eternal, unchanging God remains steadfast. He is the same yesterday, today, and forever. But to trust and believe this way requires an intimate personal knowledge of the character of God. For you cannot trust whom you do not know.

If we believe in the magnificent names of God, if we trust in the unchanging character of God, if we trust in Jesus, we must let go of fear and doubt and dare to trust.

The good news is, now you know Him! Now I know Him. Now *we* know Him! Together we have learned that it's easier to walk through a trial with an all-knowing, all-loving, all-powerful God than to walk through a trial alone with a God we barely know.

When you feel unworthy, remember *Elohim* handcrafted you with great beauty to accomplish great things for His kingdom.

When you feel like no one sees or notices you, remember and wait expectantly because *El Roi* has His ever watchful eye upon you.

When that ominous mountain looms before you, stand firm and remember *El Elyon* is even higher.

When you are anxious, remember *Jehovah Shalom* promises that peace like a river will flow through you.

When you feel abandoned and forgotten, remember and soak in your *Abba Father*'s love.

Do you get the picture?

Oh, how I have loved getting to know my Father so deeply, meeting Him and connecting in fresh ways with Him as:

- *Elohim*
- *El Roi*
- *Jehovah Rapha*
- *Jehovah Nissi*
- *Jehovah Shalom*
- *Jealous, an All-Consuming Fire*
- *El Elyon*
- *Abba Father*

But there is more—so much more! My heart hungers to discover more of the heart of my God—to know, as much as I am able, the very depths of the heart of God as revealed in even more of His names:

- *Adonai* (Lord, Master)
- *El Elohe Yisrael* (Holy One of Israel)
- *El Olam* (The Everlasting God)
- *El Shaddai* (God Almighty)
- *Immanuel* (God with Us)
- *I Am*
- *Jehovah Jireh* (The Lord Will Provide)
- *Yahweh* (Lord)

- *Jehovah Sabaoth* (The Lord of Hosts)

- *Strong Tower*

- *Fortress*

- *Rock*

- *Shield*

- *Jehovah Rohi* (The Lord is My Shepherd)

- *Jehovah Shammah* (The Lord Is There)

- *Jehovah Tsidkenu* (The Lord Our Righteousness)

- *Shophet* (Judge)

Sweet friend, do you long for the same?

Just because our study together ends here, it doesn't mean *yours* has to end. God has spoken much along our journey together; let us search for more! May our Teacher take us deeper still with Him.

Until we see Him face-to-face, may the cry of our hearts be, "We want *more* of You, Father. Please give us more of You!"

Optional Video Study

Use the space below to note anything that stands out to you from the video teaching. You may also choose to take notes on a separate sheet of paper.

Use the following questions as a guide for group discussion:

What one thing stood out to you most in this chapter?

How can you apply the name of God you studied this week to your own life and current situation?

Take a few moments to review this week's memory verse together. What does this verse mean to you personally?

Could you relate to any of the people or situations from the Bible that you studied this week? If so, how?

⇢Endnotes⇠

Chapter 1

[1] *New Strong's Expanded Exhaustive Concordance of the Bible* (Nashville: Thomas Nelson, 2001), #1254.

[2] Ibid., #8414.

[3] Ibid., #922.

[4] Ibid., #2821 and #2822.

[5] Ibid., #4327.

[6] Ibid., #6754.

[7] Ibid., #1823.

[8] A.W. Tozer, *The Pursuit of God*, special ed. (Carol Stream, Ill.: Tyndale House Publishers), 21.

[9] Ibid.

[10] Ibid., 22.

[11] *New Strong's Expanded Exhaustive Concordance of the Bible*, #4161.

[12] Ibid., #6754.

[13] Ibid., #1823.

[14] Wayne Grudem, *Bible Doctrine: Essential Teachings of the Christian Faith* (Grand Rapids: Zondervan, 1999), 104.

[15] http://en.wikipedia.org/wiki/Nicene_Creed.

[16] Warren W. Wiersbe, *The Bible Exposition Commentary* (Bellingham, Wash.: Logos).

Chapter 2

[1] *New Strong's Expanded Exhaustive Concordance of the Bible*, #1877.

[2] Ibid., #4999.

[3] http://www.freebiblecommentary.org/old_testament_studies/VOL09BOT/VOL09BOT_103.html.

[4] *New Strong's Expanded Exhaustive Concordance of the Bible*, #4166.

[5] Lisa has given me permission to share her story.

Chapter 3

[1] *Matthew Henry's Commentary on the Whole Bible: Complete and Unabridged In One Volume*, Numbers 2:1–2 (Peabody, Mass.: Hendrickson, 2008).

[2] *New Strong's Expanded Exhaustive Concordance of the Bible*, #3525.

[3] Ibid., #1127.

[4] Warren W. Wiersbe, *The Bible Exposition Commentary*, 1 Peter 5:8 (Wheaton, Ill.: Victor Books, 1996).

[5] Anne Graham Lotz, *Just Give Me Jesus* (Nashville: W Publishing, 2000), 199.

[6] Roger Ellsworth, *Opening Up Joshua* (Bellingham, Wash.: Logos).

Chapter 4

[1] Mary Beth Chapman, *Choosing to See* (Grand Rapids: Revell, 2010), 254.

[2] Ibid., 255.

[3] *Matthew Henry's Commentary on the Whole Bible: Complete and Unabridged In One Volume*, Exodus 14:22–27.

[4] Warren W. Wiersbe, *Wiersbe's Expository Outlines on the Old Testament*, 2 Kings 20:1–11 (Bellingham, Wash.: Logos).

[5] Chapman, 450–451.

[6] *New Strong's Expanded Exhaustive Concordance of the Bible*, #7495.

[7] Ibid., #2483 and #4341.

[8] Ibid., #2192, #2560, and #3554.

[9] Ibid., #1411.

[10] Ibid., #1784.

[11] Ibid., #2296.

Chapter 5

[1] http://www.therefinersfire.org/meaning_of_shalom.htm.

[2] Elisabeth Elliot, *Keep a Quiet Heart* (Ann Arbor: Vine Books, 1995), 58–59.

[3] Ibid.

[4] *The Teacher's Bible Commentary* (26), F. H. Paschall and H. H. Hobbs, eds. (Nashville: Broadman and Holman, 1972).

[5] J. M. Freeman and H. J. Chadwick, *Manners and Customs of the Bible* (537) (North Brunswick, N.J.: Bridge-Logos Publishers, 1998).

[6] *New Strong's Expanded Exhaustive Concordance of the Bible*, #5206.

[7] David Jeremiah, *The Book of Romans, Volume III*, Romans 8 (San Diego: Turning Point, 2000), 41.

[8] K. S. Wuest, *Wuest's Word Studies from the Greek New Testament: For the English Reader*, Mark 14:36 (Grand Rapids: Eerdmans, 1997).

[9] Jeremiah, 43.

[10] Henry Blackaby and Claude King, *Experiencing God* (Nashville: Lifeway, 2001), 42.

[11] From an interview with the Billy Graham Evangelistic Association, http://billygraham.org/story/henry-blackaby-still-experiencing-god/.

Proverbs 31
MINISTRIES

About Proverbs 31 Ministries

If you were inspired by *I Know His Name* and desire to deepen your own personal relationship with Jesus Christ, I encourage you to connect with Proverbs 31 Ministries.

Proverbs 31 Ministries exists to be a trusted friend who will take you by the hand and walk by your side, leading you one step closer to the heart of God through:

- free online daily devotions

- COMPEL writing community

- daily radio program

- books and resources

- online Bible studies

- free mobil device app that delivers a 5-minute daily Bible study first thing in the morning

To learn more about Proverbs 31 Ministries, call 877-731-4663 or visit www.Proverbs31.org.

Proverbs 31 Ministries
630 Team Rd., Suite 100
Matthews, NC 28105
www.Proverbs31.org